PSYCHIC
EMPOWERMENT
FOR HEALTH AND FITNESS

ABOUT PSYCHIC EMPOWERMENT FOR HEALTH AND FITNESS:

"Joe Slate has done it again! The fruit of over 30 years of research in paranormal phenomena, *Psychic Empowerment for Health and Fitness* is the handbook for thinking your way to better health in the 21st century."

— *Dr. Penne J. Laubenthal*
Athens State College

"Integrates traditional health and fitness concepts into a psychic approach that is realistic and workable. From managing weight to slowing aging, from interacting with angels to drawing power from nature, this book uncovers vast new sources of strength and power."

— *Magdi S. Tadros, Ph.D.*
Professor of Psychology and Languages, Wallace State College

"A clearly defined aid to living a joyful existence of wellness, acceptance of self and others as oneness with the Universal Power."

— *Mary J. White, Msc.D., Ph.D., HPh.D.*

"A gold mine of information for those of us on the path to healing ourselves and our planet."

— *Peggy M. Huddleston, M.D.*

"An immensely timely, important and useful contribution, addressing the relationship between body, mind, and spirit. It is a reference 'must' for those willing to access and be empowered by inner and outer potentials for the healing and well-being of self and others."

— *Rev. Doris M. McCafferty*
Unity Church on the Mountain

"Dr. Joe Slate shows that by engaging psychic self-empowerment strategies, it is possible to reach the untapped resources of our minds to responsibly create our own realities, including health and fitness.

— *Michael S. DeVore, M.D.*

"Having practiced many of Slate's methods, I can personally vouch for their benefit. Here Joe Slate is at his warm, accessible, and brilliant best."

— *Dr. Jane J. Barr, Ph.D.*

"Now that our society has realized that powerful spiritual experiences—even seemingly paranormal ones—are quite common, it is time we move on to publicizing techniques with which people can enter alternate states of awareness for purposes of spiritual and emotional growth. Dr. Slate has written an excellent guidebook for this purpose."

— *Raymond A. Moody, M.D., Ph.D.*

"Dr. Slate offers a wide assortment of spiritual and psychic methods to choose from for everyone who seeks greater health empowerment."

— *Dr. Robert Buck Goyer*
Ordained Minister

"Offers a totally new approach to health and fitness. Drawing from his extensive clinical experience, Dr. Slate offers sound, workable strategies that focus on a wide range of health issues, integrating conventional and non-conventional concepts into a bold new model of health and fitness."

— *R. Bryan Kennedy, Ed.D.*

ABOUT THE AUTHOR

Joe H. Slate is a licensed psychologist and founder of the International Parapsychology Research Foundation. He is Professor Emeritus at Athens State College, Alabama, where he served as Head of the Division of Behavioral Sciences, and Director of Institutional Effectiveness. He is Honorary Professor at Montevallo University and Adjunct Professor at Forest Institute of Professional Psychology. After completing his Ph.D. at the University of Alabama, Dr. Slate punctuated his training with additional study in hypnosis and somatoform disorders at the University of California. His research interests, while focusing on psychic empowerment, have involved him in a wide range of health-related studies, including stress management, wellness, pain management, and rejuvenation. Dr. Slate's research has been funded by the U. S. Army Missile Research and Development Command, Huntsville, Alabama; the Parapsychology Foundation, New York City; and numerous private sources.

TO WRITE TO THE AUTHOR

If you wish to contact the author or would like more information about this book, please write to the author in care of Llewellyn Worldwide, and we will forward your request. Both the author and publisher appreciate hearing from you and learning of your enjoyment of this book and how it has helped you. Llewellyn Worldwide cannot guarantee that every letter written to the author can be answered, but all will be forwarded. Please write to:

Llewellyn's New Worlds of Mind and Spirit
P.O. Box 64383, Dept. K634-3, St. Paul, MN 55164-0383, U.S.A.
Please enclose a self-addressed, stamped envelope for reply, or $1.00 to
cover costs. If outside U.S.A., enclose international postal reply coupon.

FREE CATALOG FROM LLEWELLYN

For more than ninety years Llewellyn has brought its readers knowledge in the fields of metaphysics and human potential. Learn about the newest books in spiritual guidance, natural healing, astrology, occult philosophy, and more. Enjoy book reviews, New Age articles, a calendar of events, plus current advertised products and services. To get your free copy of Llewellyn's New Worlds, send your name and address to:

Llewellyn's New Worlds of Mind and Spirit
P.O. Box 64383, Dept. K634-3, St. Paul, MN 55164-0383, U.S.A.
Please enclose a self-addressed, stamped envelope for reply, or $1.00 to
cover costs. If outside U.S.A., enclose international postal reply coupon.

Llewellyn's Strategies for Success Series

PSYCHIC
EMPOWERMENT
FOR HEALTH AND FITNESS

JOE SLATE, PH.D.

1996
Llewellyn Publications
P.O. Box 64383, Dept. K634-3
St. Paul, Minnesota 55164-0383, U.S.A.

FIRST EDITION
First Printing, 1996

Cover Design: Tom Grewe
Cover Image: Digital Stock Corporation
Photography: Charles Seifried Photography
Book Design and Layout: Designed To Sell

Library of Congress Cataloging-in-Publication Data
Slate, Joe H.
     Psychic empowerment for health and fitness / Joe H. Slate.
          p.   cm. — (Strategies for success)
     Includes index.
     ISBN 1-56718-634-3 (trade paperback : alk. paper)
     1. Mental Healing. 2. Autogenic training. 3. Success—Psychic aspects. 4. Self-help techniques. 5. Self-efficacy.   I. Title.   II. Series.
   RZ401.S64   1996
     158'.1—dc20   96-12237
                                                                         CIP

Llewellyn Publications
A Division of Llewellyn Worldwide, Ltd.
P.O. Box 64383, Dept. K634-3
St. Paul, Minnesota 55164-0383, U.S.A.

ABOUT LLEWELLYN'S STRATEGIES FOR SUCCESS SERIES

The secret to success is really no secret at all. Just ask any successful person. The "secret" is really a universal truth that belongs to each and every human being on the planet. That truth is: Success begins in the Mind.

Many of us live from day to day feeling that "something" is missing, or that we are a victim of circumstances that make success impossible.

The greatest barrier to success is this illusion of helplessness and powerlessness. It is the illusion that you have no choices in life. The successful person knows that this illusion is like a deadly virus to the spirit.

The good news is that you possess the power—inside yourself now—to sweep illusions from your mind and begin using your mind for what it was intended: to lift human consciousness to a higher plane and make this planet a better place for yourself and your children.

How is this done?

That's where Llewellyn's Strategies for Success come in. Techniques are available that can help you activate your inner resources to create exciting new potentials in your life. Some of these techniques involve the promotion of psychic empowerment.

Psychic empowerment concepts and strategies recognize that the source of ultimate power resides within the Mind. Whether a simple affirmation or a complex empowering procedure, each strategy embodies a firm regard for the divine spark of greatness existing in everyone.

Your psychic faculties are standing behind the door of consciousness. With the techniques presented in this book, you can open the door and enjoy a success beyond your wildest dreams.

Success is your destiny. When you are self-empowered, you become the sole architect of your life. Why wait? Seize your power now.

OTHER BOOKS BY THE AUTHOR

Psychic Phenomena: New Principles,
Techniques and Applications (McFarland)

Self-Empowerment: Strategies for Success (Colonial Press)

Psychic Empowerment: A 7-Day Plan for Self-Development
(Llewellyn)

FORTHCOMING

A Psychic Empowerment Guide to Out-of-Body Experiences

A Psychic Empowerment Guide to Clairvoyance

A Psychic Empowerment Guide to Dowsing and Divination

A Psychic Empowerment Guide to Crystal Gazing

A Psychic Empowerment Guide to Career Success

DEDICATION

To all who choose growth, knowledge, and change.

TABLE OF CONTENTS

LIST OF ILLUSTRATIONS

ACKNOWLEDGMENTS

I am indebted to many people who influenced the writing of this book. I am especially grateful to the many students who shared their experiences with me, and who volunteered to participate in my research efforts. Many of them are far ahead of their time. They have enriched my life, and I feel honored to have known them.

I owe a special debt of gratitude to my learned colleagues who offered invaluable suggestions and encouragement throughout the course of this project. Many of the concepts of psychic empowerment found in this book are the products of countless hours of collaboration with men and women who are giants in their fields.

I am especially grateful to the International Parapsychology Research Foundation for its unwavering support and encouragement. Established at Athens State College, Alabama, in 1970, the Foundation has sponsored a continual flow of psychical research that provided the empirical basis for many of the health and fitness strategies presented for the first time in this book.

INTRODUCTION

This book offers a fresh, new way of looking at health and fitness. It systematically develops the psychic-empowerment model of health and fitness, introducing a vast range of new possibilities for promoting our physical and mental well-being. Although the book focuses on our inner capacities for health and fitness, it recognizes the relevance of outer dimensions and higher planes of power. It views a healthful, empowered lifestyle as a reasonable expectation for everyone.

The psychic-empowerment model provides a totally new framework, which integrates an array of important health and fitness concepts into an innovative, psychic approach. It offers laboratory-tested, step-by-step strategies, while taking into account the physical, mental, and spiritual nature of our being. From managing weight to slowing aging, from interacting with angels to empowering the globe, it guides us toward newer, more efficient ways of enriching our lives, while at the same time, empowering us to bring forth positive change in the world.

The psychic-empowerment model of health and fitness is a dynamic, interactive approach. It emphasizes the power of the mind to probe the innermost part of the self and the highest dimensions of reality. It challenges us to untangle the many mysteries of the universe, and to discover new meaning in our existence. The psychic-empowerment model views our existence as purposeful and growth-driven. We are not here by accident, but by design. Each moment, we chart our voyage and shape our destiny, and are responsible for our development and the quality of our lives.

The first part of this book focuses on the abundance of our inner potentials, and on our capacity to activate them for health and fitness. The book then explores other dimensions of power, and develops strategies to engage these dimensions in a variety of health-enhancing interactions. The final section of the book presents "A Seven-Day Health and Fitness Plan," designed to initiate an upward spiral of mental and physical empowerment. A major emphasis throughout the book is on workable concepts and proven strategies.

We have come a long way in our quest for knowledge and understanding. We have learned more about our mental, physical, and spiritual nature in the past decade than in the past century. Yet, we have scarcely begun to comprehend the magnitude and magnificence of our existence. The future is challenging and filled with promise. This book offers not only a new approach, but also a bright glimpse of the boundless possibilities.

❧ I ❧

THE PSYCHIC-EMPOWERMENT MODEL OF HEALTH AND FITNESS

Today, worldwide interest in health and fitness is at an all-time high. With the cloud of killer viruses and other health threats looming ominously on the horizon, physicians, social workers, psychologists, teachers, nutritionists, and health and fitness specialists everywhere stress the importance of maintaining health and preventing illness. Contemporary programs emphasize the value of a healthy diet, exercise, safe sexual practices, and of course, preventive health care and appropriate medical treatment. A healthy, empowered lifestyle, not only in the formative years but throughout life, is recognized as essential to our mental and physical well-being. Increasingly, psychological factors, such as a positive mental state and good self-image, are emphasized as critical variables affecting our health and fitness.

As a result of unprecedented medical progress and a rising health consciousness, we are living longer. Unfortunately, our biological systems do not always keep pace with our longevity. New and creative approaches are needed if we are to make the best of our lives and maximize the quality of our existence. The starting point must be a multi-faceted strategy which recognizes traditional advances, but does not exclude the potential benefits of new, empowering concepts. Such an approach requires a dramatic change in our thinking, and a heightened awareness of the power of the mind to shape our health destiny.

All too often, negative mental elements dominate our lives. The long-term results are a deterioration in our functioning efficiency and, in some instances, destructive biological or structural change. Given time, negative states such as smoldering hostility, feelings of inferiority, low self-esteem, and loss of self-worth wear down our adaptive resources, and weaken the fragile circuitry of the central nervous system. We become vulnerable and disempowered, both mentally and physically. The focus of our energies is interrupted, and the quality of our social relations, family life, and career progressively declines. For the severely disempowered, performing even routine, daily tasks becomes difficult; and, the longer the duration of disempowerment, the greater the loss of empowering resources, which makes the recovery process all the more difficult.

In behavioral medicine, the introduction of new wonder drugs has significantly advanced the effectiveness of modern treatment programs. Mental-health specialists concede, however, that certain, menacing serpents lurk in the psychopharmaceutical garden. Among them are the side-effects of many of these drugs, and the potential for drug dependency. An even greater danger is that we all too often come to believe there is little or nothing we can do for ourselves. The psychic-empowerment model of health and fitness, as presented in this book, attacks this attitude of helplessness, and offers a myriad of self-empowering options with far-reaching implications.

This model for health and fitness must logically include an emphasis on the physical body and its needs. Good nutrition, exercise, rest, and recreation are critical constants of a healthy lifestyle; but even with these essentials in place, our health and the quality of our lives, can be enhanced though a better understanding of the mind and its empowering potentials. For instance, an optimistic state of mind, an unsinkable spirit, a sense of humor, and a positive attitude all promote health. They empower the body's immune system and bolster our resistance to disease. It is now evident that we can literally *think* ourselves to better health.

Even though recent medical progress has resulted in evidence linking key emotional states to good physical health; a neglected, but critical area of health and fitness remains: the relationship between our psychic faculties and our physical and mental well-being. Central to the psychic-empowerment model is a recognition of that interaction and the phenomenal power of the mind to initiate it. Unsurpassed in its complexity, and unparalleled in its power, the mind is capable not only of influencing itself, but of intervening directly into critical biological processes to extinguish destructive elements and introduce constructive functions to promote health and wellness.

At first glance, such an empowered state seems almost too good to be true; but a closer look reveals possibilities which are greater still. Each of us is an intricately complex system—physically, mentally, psychically, and spiritually. Until now, we have barely tinkered at the edges of the mind's psychic powers. Among the exciting possibilities is an extensive range of health and fitness benefits: reversing stress-related structural damage, strengthening the enfeebled central nervous system, restoring normal cerebral blood flow, accelerating healing, managing pain, fortifying the body's defense systems, and slowing or even reversing the aging process. Our psychic resources can be applied to break unwanted habits, extinguish phobias, increase creativity, accelerate learning, improve memory, master sports and artistic skills, and increase intellectual efficiency; and these are only a few of the psychic empowerment possibilities within our reach.

The psychic-empowerment model of health and fitness recognizes the basic psychic nature of all human beings. Each psychic experience is a confirmation of power residing within the self. That power frequently manifests itself through some form of extrasensory perception (ESP) such as telepathy, or the psychic sending and receiving of thought messages; clairvoyance, involving the psychic awareness of situations or conditions; and precognition, the psychic awareness of future events. Whatever the nature of its manifestation, ESP can no longer be dismissed as inconsequential, or simply another form of sensory experience. ESP, unlike sensory perception, functions beyond our thresholds for *sensory* experience, at both conscious and subconscious levels of awareness, enriching our lives with exciting new knowledge and understanding.

Empowering psychic phenomena are not limited to ESP, however; other manifestations of our psychic nature include psychokinesis (PK), or the direct capacity of the mind to influence movement and matter; out-of-body experiences (OBEs), or the awareness of being at a spatial location separate from the physical body; and discarnate phenomena such as the near-death experience (NDE) and interactions with discarnate dimensions (sightings, channeling, and mediumship). These experiences often are accompanied by enlightenment, self-illumination, and a clear awareness of higher planes of power.

Despite the many profound manifestations of our psychic faculties, most of our psychic experiences involve common, everyday situations such as a dream that comes true, the intuitive solution to a problem, a psychic message spontaneously received from a friend or relative, a flash of precognitive insight, or the comforting awareness of a guiding, angelic presence. Without exception, the psychic experience is purposeful, though its purpose may simply be to provide practical information or insight to enrich our lives and promote our growth. We are a work in progress, not a finished product, and the psychic experience can increase our awareness of opportunities around us, inspiring us to make the best of our lives. On the other hand, it can also invoke significant issues of life and death. Given precognitive awareness, we can avert danger, avoid accidents, or prepare for fateful events beyond our control. Even PK, while often spontaneous and seemingly uncontrolled, can affect matters of physical survival. A mountain climber, for instance, escaped injury in a fall, when she mentally enveloped her body in a protective bubble of air. She immediately felt warm energy surrounding her body, slowing the fall and cushioning its impact.

The psychic-empowerment model recognizes the relevance of both conscious and subconscious regions of the mind. Many of our psychic potentials, including those relating to health and fitness, appear to reside in the subconscious. A greater understanding of that rich, inner reservoir, and skill in exploiting its untapped resources, could improve our psychic effectiveness and appreciably enrich our lives.

Clearly, our psychic make-up and each psychic function—conscious and subconscious—equip us with valuable resources for mental and physical empowerment. Even in underdeveloped, spontaneous forms, these powerful assets promote our well-being. Developing and *deliberately* using them could greatly expand our possibilities for an empowered, fulfilled life.

Although the strategies developed in this book focus primarily on personal health and fitness, many of them involve skills which could be applied to other important goals. Self-hypnosis, for instance, is not only useful as a health and physical fitness tool, it can also be used to build self-esteem, improve problem-solving skills, dissolve growth blockages, generate insight, and resolve conflict. Out-of-body techniques, rather than being limited to health-related issues, have wide-ranging applications, such as gathering information, increasing awareness, and stimulating creative thinking. Health strategies associated with the human aura, dreams, crystal gazing, and the pyramid can be readily adapted to an almost unlimited range of personal empowerment goals.

Psychic phenomena also have empowering relevance on a global scale. Our psychic faculties can tap into new global resources and make connections around the world. They can be applied to help solve some of the world's most pressing problems. World peace, as an example, must eventually flow, not from the systematic killing of our own kind, but from constructive efforts and collective psychic energies generated by people committed to harmony and peace, rather than conflict and war. Urgent global issues such as hunger, violence, pollution, and depletion of our natural resources, demand our involvement in generating fresh, innovative approaches. Psychic intervention could uncover corrective and preventive strategies for saving this planet, and for making it a safer place for ourselves and our children. Solving these widespread global problems is essential to a healthy global environment. For instance, we are running out of clean water. A solution to this problem would benefit everyone, now and in the future; but achieving many of our global objectives requires a cooperative effort and powerful energies generated on a global scale—a process in which each of us becomes a critical contributor. Such a task is daunting, but not impossible. Our global and personal empowerment goals can be achieved through techniques we can implement individually and collectively. A major aim of this book is to provide workable strategies and new approaches to enriching our lives, while contributing to a better world.

Finally, the psychic-empowerment model of health and fitness acknowledges other dimensions of power in the universe, along with our capacity to interact with them. Like the inner self, the outer universe, by its very existence, beckons us to explore its depth and uncover its secrets. With each probe, we are awestruck by its magnitude and magnificence. Each new discovery of power in the universe is a celebration of the power within the self; and together, the inner dimensions of the self and the outer dimensions of the universe willingly yield their empowering resources, while challenging us to explore further. The strategies presented in this book respond to the challenge by accessing and activating the innermost powers of the self, and the outermost powers of the universe, to enrich our lives mentally, physically, and spiritually.

2

Self-Hypnosis: Accessing Inner Power

Hypnosis is one of the most important empowering tools of modern times. When appropriately used, it can connect us to the deepest subconscious regions of the self and activate a vast inner reserve of power. Hypnosis is a critical component in our psychic-empowerment model of health and fitness because it offers a framework for accessing and developing our psychic skills. It dissolves growth blockages, liberates hidden resources, and generates an empowered state conducive to our mental and physical well-being.

The empowering possibilities of hypnosis have been recognized, if only indirectly, since ancient times. Many primitive rituals, remnants of which have survived to this day as cultural rites, appear to have been designed to induce a trance-like state in which superhuman feats could be performed, or certain magical powers could be manifested. Some of these rituals, including those preceding battle, were ingenuously designed to generate certain preparatory or post-ritual effects, such as increased physical prowess, or bravery in the face of danger or death.

In recent years, the use of hypnosis to unlock the empowering potentials of the mind has been gaining acceptance and recognition from medical and behavioral scientists alike. Contemporary interest in hypnosis typically has centered on its usefulness in facilitating the achievement of personal goals, such as controlling weight, breaking habits, managing stress, building self-esteem, overcoming fear, and improving creativity, learning, and memory. At the cutting edge of this technology are the many bright, promising applications of hypnosis to affect the physical body, such as in controlling pain, accelerating healing, and strengthening the body's defense and immune systems. Hypnosis can empower us to make the best of our lives—to live better, healthier, and perhaps, longer. Theoretically, hypnosis could slow brain aging by stimulating nerve growth factors either to form new nerve connections or to reform old ones. The results could be a healthier, younger brain, and a happier, longer life.

Once called "the handmaiden of mysticism," hypnosis has been shrouded in mystery and controversy. This may be due in part to the complexity of the trance state and the spontaneous effects that often accompany it. Psychic functions, such as extrasensory perception and out-of-body experiences, sometimes are exacerbated during the trance state. Frequently, the subject of hypnosis will slip into a "past-life state," and experience previously unexplored dimensions of the self. Occasionally and inexplicably, hypnosis will generate new, full-blown skills. This phenomenon, sometimes called "hypnoproduction," literally can create new talents and proficiencies, such as the immediate command of a new language or the mastery of a musical or artistic skill. Many important social and scientific advances have been attributed to insight generated during the trance state.

THE NATURE OF HYPNOSIS

Although clinical researchers generate a constant stream of new knowledge about this empowering tool, many misconceptions linger concerning the nature of hypnosis. The psychic-empowerment perspective views hypnosis as an altered state of consciousness, in which receptivity to suggestion is heightened. Clinicians who use the procedure, however, vary in their definitions and descriptions of the hypnotic experience. For instance, some view it as a trance state, in which perceptions can be altered and controlled; whereas others view it as simply a relaxed, responsive state. Some emphasize its effectiveness in probing the subconscious, while others primarily focus on its capacity to promote behavioral change. Most clinical hypnotists agree, however, that, whatever its essential nature or true definition, hypnosis is a powerful tool with many important applications.

Our interviews with potential subjects for hypnosis, drawn from a college-student population, identified common concerns regarding the trance experience. The following are some frequently raised questions.

1. *Is hypnosis dangerous?* Hypnosis is a valuable empowerment tool for personal health and self-mastery. It can be trusted when used wisely by skilled specialists, or when practiced by oneself within suitable guidelines. Like other empowerment tools, hypnosis can be harmful if used unwisely, or practiced by the untrained. Any adverse effect is almost always the result of either faulty suggestions or inappropriate management procedures. The potential risks of hypnosis are minimized by training and proper safeguards, including clear, positive objectives formed prior to hypnosis; a quiet, safe, trance setting free of interruption or distraction; and

goal-oriented hypnotic suggestions and affirmations presented in positive terms.

2. *Can I be hypnotized?* Everyone is hypnotizable, but the degree of susceptibility to hypnosis varies widely among subjects. Concentration abilities, imagery skills, and responsiveness to suggestion are among the characteristics that facilitate the induction process. We use these skills in our daily lives, and much of our daily experience is spontaneously registered in our subconscious, or stored as neural connections, capable of later activating thoughts, feelings, or actions. Becoming lost in thought or absorbed in a book or movie, day-dreaming, and simply reminiscing are examples of hypnotic-like experiences familiar to everyone. Also, when falling asleep, we all experience a brief state of altered awareness, similar to hypnosis, called "hypnagogic sleep," This sleep stage is characterized by dream-like images and increased receptivity to suggestion. Thoughts and images generated in that stage can influence, not only sleep and dreaming, but waking behavior as well. In Chapter Five, we will discuss ways of arresting the hypnogogic stage of sleep, and using it as a hypnotic-like trance to empower our lives.

3. *Once hypnotized, how deeply will I go?* The trance state exists on a continuum of awareness and receptivity. The levels of hypnosis range from a very light trance state of increased receptivity, to a profound state of altered consciousness, where perceptions can be controlled and subconscious levels of awareness and experience accessed. Heightened or decreased awareness and alterations in perceptual functioning can be experienced at trance levels of various depths, however.

Like the induction process itself, deepening the trance state to the desired level involves concentration, imagery, and receptivity to suggestion. Although a few beginning subjects will reach the deepest, somnambulant-like level of hypnosis, the majority will experience a relaxing, light-to-moderate trance state sufficient for most health and physical-fitness applications, including tension and anxiety reduction, pain management, and the alleviation of physical symptoms of stress. Highly practical applications such as breaking unwanted habits, weight management, improved motivation, building self-esteem, and enhanced learning, likewise can be accomplished in the light-to-moderate trance state. A deeper level of hypnosis usually is required for applications such as recovering memories buried deep in the subconscious, and resolving subconscious conflicts underlying physical and psychological symptoms. Applications such as age-regression (recovery of past-life experiences) typically require a profound trance state. Achieving such a deep trance level in self-hypnosis usually requires strong motivation, and practice with a variety of induction and deepening techniques.

4. *Can I be hypnotized against my will?* The first step in successful hypnosis is giving yourself permission to enter the trance state. Of course you are unlikely to attempt self-hypnosis in the absence of intent to enter the trance state; but despite such intent, whether in hypnosis or self-hypnosis, subconscious resistance can disrupt efforts to achieve the desired level of trance. Expressing permission and intent minimizes this resistance. In self-hypnosis, post-hypnotic suggestions such as:

> *In the future, I will enter the trance state with confidence and ease, and I am increasing my capacity to respond to trance-induction procedures*

are usually effective in facilitating future induction efforts, and overcoming subconscious resistance.

5. *Will I do something irrational or embarrassing while in hypnosis?* Although inhibitions may be lowered during the trance state, the same social and moral restraints characterizing normal, waking life remain essentially in place. Hypnosis is not a surrender of the will, but an affirmation of the power of the mind. Each suggestion and affirmation presented during the trance state is effective only when it has met with the mind's consent. Hypnosis cannot bring about positive change in an unwilling subject.

6. *How can I be certain that I will come out of the trance state?* This question is raised often by subjects who resist hypnosis out of concern that they could experience difficulty exiting the trance, and retain some adverse, residual baggage from the experience. Following the trance, certain sensations, such as tingling or numbness in the hands, are common, but typically short-lived. Should such effects persist they can be removed by simply re-entering hypnosis, and restoring normal functions. Failure to respond to suggestions to end the trance is primarily due to resistance, and can result in a brief continuation of the trance. This can be prevented through a simple suggestion presented early in the trance:

> *I will come out of hypnosis at any moment by simply deciding to do so.*

The trance state, particularly when practiced in the evening, will occasionally give way to sleep, and hypnosis can be very effective in inducing restful sleep and peaceful dreaming.

7. *Will I remember what happened during the trance?* Our recall of trance contents can be influenced by both trance depth and the nature of trance suggestions. With the exception of deep-trance contents, recall is typically quite complete. Deeper trance experiences may result in recall which is either sketchy or lost altogether; however, appropriate post-hypnotic suggestions lasting beyond the trance state, can ensure complete, detailed recall. At deep levels, post-hypnotic suggestions can also be formulated to extinguish all recall of trance contents, or to provide recall of certain selected trance experiences only. For most goal-related applications of self-hypnosis, total recall is preferred, because it facilitates motivation and goal achievement. In self-hypnosis, such full recall is ensured by the simple post-hypnotic suggestion:

> *Upon coming out of hypnosis, I will have full and complete recall of all that I experienced during the trance state.*

Some analytical applications of self-hypnosis are best served by *limited* awareness and recall. Repressions buried in the subconscious (including past-life trauma) yield reluctantly to hypnotic probes, because the distress of such experiences could overwhelm the conscious mind. In self-hypnosis, these analytic probes should be used with caution. Appropriate safeguards against painful, premature invasion of repressed content into consciousness are simple suggestions presented early in the trance state:

> *During hypnosis, I will experience only those contents that are empowering to me at this time. I will experience other contents when I am empowered to benefit from them.*

Should disempowering contents surface during the trance state, they can be effectively managed by these post-hypnotic suggestions:

> *I will remember only those contents which are empowering to me at this time. I will recall other contents only when I am empowered to benefit from them.*

8. **Will I be a good hypnotic subject?** Although everyone can be hypnotized, not everyone will be hypnotized at the same rate or to the same depth, whether through one's own efforts or with the assistance of a skilled hypnotist. Likewise, the effectiveness of the trance experience will vary from individual to individual. Our success at self-hypnosis depends first upon formulating clear objectives prior to hypnosis, and second upon applying appropriate induction, deepening, and trance-management techniques.

For most health and fitness goals, self-hypnosis, rather than hypnosis, is the preferred strategy, because the induction procedure itself exercises the mind's capacity to influence the physical body. Self-hypnosis, also called auto-hypnosis, is a self-induced trance state where receptivity to auto-suggestion is heightened. In that state, attention, sensation, and perception are managed exclusively by the self; the choosing self is the sole executive in command of the trance experience. In hypnosis, the *hypnotist* executes the induction process and directs the trance event. In a sense, however, all hypnosis is self-hypnosis, for in the absence of the responsive, choosing self, a trance state will not occur.

The basic skills associated with self-hypnosis and other self-empowerment strategies are remarkably similar. Physical relaxation, command of subconscious processes, a positive mental state, empowering mental imagery, and positive affirmations are critical variables underlying most psychic growth and empowerment strategies, including self-hypnosis. Among the spontaneous effects of these are an abundance of health and fitness benefits. These benefits are maximized, however, by the direct, deliberate application of strategies to access and liberate inner sources of health and fitness.

Self-hypnosis, as an empowering strategy, is based on the premise that within the self lies a vast wealth of latent potential awaiting activation to enrich and empower our lives. Some of this potential exists in conscious regions, readily accessible through conscious efforts. Some, however, exists in hidden, subconscious regions, and is typically accessible only through strategies which probe that vast region.

Most of us develop only a small percentage of our total potential during our lifetime. Much of the remaining reservoir of growth possibilities, including dormant resources for health and fitness, remains in the subconscious. If we tap into that hidden part of the self, we can initiate a growth spiral to liberate these potentials, and literally create new growth possibilities. With that new surge of inner power, we could unlock the door of the mind, and become the master of our lives—with amazing results.

HEALTH AND FITNESS
APPLICATIONS FOR HYPNOSIS

Self-hypnosis is a goal-directed and growth-oriented strategy. Its effectiveness as a health and fitness tool requires a mastery of trance-induction and management procedures with varying effectiveness for achieving particular goals. In fact, the complexity of the mind and the uniqueness of the dynamics underlying various applications of self-hypnosis, has stymied attempts to develop a trance procedure suitable for all purposes. Consequently, self-empowerment applications of hypnosis demand a repertoire of specialties, each tailored to a particular health or fitness goal.

Notwithstanding the variety of trance procedures, and the uniqueness of each trace experience, certain conditions are common to all applications of self-hypnosis. The physical setting must be safe and free of distractions, and a period of approximately one hour should be allocated for the typical session. Needless to say, self-hypnosis should never be attempted while driving an automobile, operating machinery, or under any condition involving risk or danger. Aside from the physical setting, a motivated state with clearly specified objectives, along with positive expectations of success, invariably facilitates the induction process, and maximizes the benefits of self-hypnosis. Hypnotic affirmations should be presented as concise, positive statements of fact, in the first person. They can be spoken aloud or expressed mentally. (Although audio tapes and various mechanical induction aids are commercially available, the most effective procedures are those we implement for ourselves.)

Success with self-hypnosis depends not only upon trance induction and deepening skills, but also upon our effectiveness in *managing* the trance state. Trance management requires practice, and a mastery of skills with which to access inner powers and awaken dormant potentials. The use of self-hypnosis to achieve personal goals essentially consists of the following three steps:

1. *Goal formulation.* Prior to hypnosis, clearly identify the purpose of the trance experience. Be specific and positive. If your goal, for instance, is to lose weight, specify the amount of weight, and affirm your intent and ability to achieve that goal. Be bold and adventurous as you explore your deeper self; your dormant, inner potentials await your probes, and will readily respond to positive, goal-related suggestions and affirmations.

2. *Trance induction.* Select a trance-induction procedure which seems right for your purpose. If your goal is to become more relaxed and in command of situations around you, a relaxation-induction procedure could integrate your goals into the induction procedure itself. On the other hand, if your goal is to build your creative powers, the innovative, "Star Gaze" induction procedure, as discussed later in this chapter, could induce a state of readiness, and activate your creative potentials.

3. *Trance management.* Once a trance state of sufficient depth has been achieved, reaffirm your previously formulated goals, and implement your strategies to achieve them. The trance experience, while itself typically rewarding, is a means to opening the door to the vast inner region of your subconscious potentials. Trance-management strategies enable you to activate those resources and effectively apply them. From lofty concerns such as self-discovery, inner-peace, and spiritual unfoldment, to basic goals such as professional success, habit control, and rejuvenation, trance-management strategies can remove blockages that thwart

your growth, and unleash powerful inner potentials to ensure your success. There is an evolving body of evidence to suggest that self-hypnosis can be applied to stimulate various psychic functions, such as extrasensory perception, psychokinesis, out-of-body travel, and enlightening interactions with higher dimensions of reality. Increasing your rate of learning, improving memory, developing athletic skills, learning new languages, and literally creating intelligence are not beyond the scope of this powerful tool.

In self-hypnosis, ending the trance state is usually initiated by simply deciding to exit hypnosis, and affirming:

I am now ready to end the trance state.

For most applications, a gradual, rather than abrupt termination of the trance is recommended, because a slower exit can facilitate deeper absorption of the goal-related suggestions. A gradual exit also provides an easy transition into wakefulness, and full resolution of the trance experience. Such an ending is facilitated by slowly counting from one to five, as suggestions of being alert, revitalized, and refreshed are presented. The counting procedure is ended with positive, post-hypnotic affirmations such as:

Upon now opening my eyes, I will be fully alert, tranquil, and secure. The suggestions I have given myself will remain deep within, growing stronger and stronger day by day.

Immediately following the trance, a period of reflection, during which the trance experiences are reviewed and the goal expectations are reaffirmed, usually will increase the empowering effects of self-hypnosis.

The following empowerment applications include appropriate trance induction, deepening, and management procedures specifically designed to achieve each health or fitness goal. The trance suggestions and affirmations can either be mentally or verbally expressed, or an audio recording of the procedures can be used if preferred; however, this approach can limit the flexibility and spontaneity of the procedure. After induction, additional deepening techniques may be applied, as needed, to maintain a trance state of sufficient depth for the duration of the procedure. Effective deepening strategies are: counting backwards while suggesting depth and drowsiness; forming relaxing mental images; and inducing various physical sensations, such as tingling, dullness, or heaviness, then carefully removing them.

STRESS MANAGEMENT

Effective stress management is one of the most valuable applications of self-hypnosis. Even moderate levels of mismanaged stress can chip away at our coping mechanisms, depleting our adjustment resources, and weakening our biological systems. The results are enfeebling and disempowering both mentally and physically. By deliberately reducing negative stress, we assume command of the critical mental and physical functions which affect the quality of our lives. The result is an empowered state that revitalize the mind and body with healthful, healing energies.

Relaxation and stress reduction are the natural by-products of many trance-induction techniques, particularly those using progressive relaxation, peaceful mental imagery, and positive affirmations. More specific stress-management procedures have been developed, however, not only to reduce existing stress levels, but also to ameliorate the consequences of prolonged stress, and strengthen our capacity to cope with future demands. It is important to note that induction approaches emphasizing relaxation, while generally effective, are known, at times, to produce the opposite effect. This ironic effect is particularly evident in people with panic disorders, who often report more intense anxiety while practicing relaxation procedures. For most self-hypnosis subjects, however, an intentional relaxation procedure, which progressively relaxes the body, is the preferred strategy.

One of the most effective strategies for managing stress is the "Cognitive Relaxation Trance Procedure." This procedure is particularly useful in combating excessive anxiety and worry, as well as extinguishing various stress-related symptoms, such as fatigue, irritability, sleep disturbance, and muscle tension. It can tap into inner psychic coping and repair mechanisms to effectively manage stress and combat its destructive physical effects. An immediate reduction in stress is often evident following a single application of this strategy.

In this procedure, the stress-management goals are integrated into the total trance experience, beginning with the induction process, and ending with the post-hypnotic suggestions. Additional affirmations related to health and fitness can be incorporated into the procedure; however, no more than three additional goals are recommended, and they should be clearly formulated prior to trance induction.

COGNITIVE RELAXATION TRANCE PROCEDURE

> To begin this procedure, assume a comfortable, reclining position, then close your eyes and slowly take a few deep breaths. Affirm your intent to enter the trance state, then develop a relaxed, rhythmic, breathing pattern, taking a

little longer to exhale. Breathe in peace and tranquillity as you breathe out stress and anxiety. Banish all negative thoughts, and let a warm glow of serenity surround you. Allow calm, peaceful imagery, perhaps of soft, fluffy clouds or a peaceful meadow, to flow spontaneously in and out of your mind. As you breathe slowly and rhythmically, let your body become more and more fully relaxed, then give yourself the following suggestions:

As I now become increasingly relaxed, all my cares are far, far away. I am quiet and at ease, secure and at peace with myself and the universe. As peaceful serenity surrounds me, I am comfortable and relaxed. Time is now slowing down as I drift deeper and deeper into relaxation. I have all the time I need to become more and more relaxed. As I soak in deep relaxation, the innermost part of my being is becoming more and more responsive to my suggestions. As relaxation moves over my body, beginning at my forehead and spreading to my feet, I will find myself drifting gently into hypnosis.

The muscles in my forehead are now deeply relaxed. The muscles are loose, and the tension is gone. Warm, soothing relaxation is now spreading gently around my eyes and over my face, soaking deeper and deeper into every muscle. Flowing downward into my neck and shoulders, relaxation is permeating every fiber. Now spreading into my arms, the relaxation is being gently absorbed into every muscle and joint. My hands are now soaking up relaxation, right into the tips of my fingers. As I become more and more comfortable, breathing slowly in and out, relaxation is soaking deeply into the muscles of my chest, in front and in back. Spreading into my abdomen, the relaxation is going deeper and deeper, right into the pit of my stomach. My hips are now soaking up relaxation, deeper and deeper into the muscles and joints. The muscles in my thighs are now relaxing, becoming increasingly loose and limp. Spreading now into the joints of my knees, the relaxation is going deeper and deeper. The muscles below my knees are now soaking up relaxation, absorbing it deeper and deeper into every fiber. Finally, my ankles and feet are soaking up soothing relaxation, deep into every muscle, joint, and tendon. My total body, from my head to the tips of my toes, is fully relaxed.

Now unfolding before me is the clear image of a deep, blue pool. (Here, allow sufficient time for vivid imagery of the pool to unfold. Focus particularly on the pool's depth and color.) *As I gaze at the pool, I am becoming increasingly relaxed, comfortable, and secure. Near the edge of the pool lies a smooth, white pebble. I now pick up the pebble and toss it into the pool, forming ripples that move gently to the water's edge.* (Again, allow sufficient time for vivid imagery to emerge. Envision the circular ripples expanding and moving outward.) *As the pebble sinks deeper and deeper, deeper and deeper into the blue pool, the ripples continue to move gently outward toward the water's edge. As I focus only on the ripples, I am now going deep, very deep into hypnosis.*

As I now count backwards from five, I will find myself going even deeper into hypnosis. Upon the count of one, I will be in a very, very deep trance state. I will be fully responsive to each of my affirmations. Five—deeper and deeper; four— very deeply relaxed; three—very deep; two— deeper and deeper; and finally, one. My mind is now responsive to my own words as I remain calm, content, and secure.

I am at complete peace with myself and the world. Day by day, I am becoming more relaxed, self-confident, and secure. All the powers of the universe are at my command. Success is my destiny. I have all the resources I need to succeed at whatever I decide to do. The solutions I need are within my reach. I can tap into them at will to empower my life, regardless of the situation around me.

Each day, I will become increasingly empowered to achieve each of my goals. (Here, specify your goals in your own words, and affirm your power to achieve them.) *My inner psychic resources are now at my command, to empower me to manage stress and combat its negative effects. The energies of health and wellness are now unleashed to flow throughout my body. Day by day, I will become healthier and happier, energized with vitality and infused with new growth potential. My inner powers are now activated. I am now ready to push forward, explore new ideas, and discover new meaning to my existence.*

The affirmations I have presented to myself are now an integral part of my innermost being. Upon coming out of hypnosis, I will have full recall of all that I have experienced in this trance state. I will remain relaxed, secure, and invigorated, filled with purpose and positive energy. I will be completely and fully empowered.

At any moment in the future, I can call forth as needed all the empowering affirmations I have given myself in this trance, by simply imaging myself tossing a pebble into a deep, blue pool, and letting myself flow with the gentle ripples.

I will now come out of hypnosis by slowly counting from one to five. Upon the count of five, I will open my eyes and be fully awake, fully alert, and fully empowered. One, two, three, four, and five.

Following the trance, a period of reflection, in which the trance's calming effects are noted and the empowerment goals are again enumerated, tends to heighten the effectiveness of the experience. This is a growth-oriented procedure and should be practiced as often as needed to maximize its empowering benefits.

WEIGHT CONTROL

With the exception of certain cultures that consider obesity a mark of beauty, Americans make up the fattest population ever to exist on this planet. The result of this epidemic is a high incidence of obesity-related illnesses, including our nation's number one killer—heart disease.

A sensible diet, proper exercise, and an empowered mental state are the essential building blocks for sound weight control and a healthy body. Weight management through self-hypnosis is designed, not simply to focus on weight control, but to raise health consciousness, and activate those dormant inner psychic resources to empower us to get the body in shape, and to keep both mind and body fit. The combination of success orientation, strong motivation, high self-esteem, empowering affirmations, related imagery, and psychic vigilance is central to weight management through self-hypnosis.

The preferred trance induction procedure for weight management is the "Hand Levitation Technique," based on a psychokinetic concept emphasizing the capacity of mental functions to induce an involuntary physical response—the levitation of the hand. Because induction through hand levitation initiates a direct mind-body interaction, the procedure is considered particularly conducive to weight-management goals, which also involve a mind-body interaction. Through selective imagery and suggestion, the hand is induced to float upward and, upon touching the forehead, to initiate a trance state in which the mind-body interaction is fully established. In the post-trance state, the empowering interaction continues unimpeded, in an inner form to facilitate weight control. This weight-management approach uses age progression as a motivation strategy, and aura imagery as a post-hypnotic cue, to activate the subconscious resources applicable to weight management. This procedure may require considerable practice, but once mastered, it is one of the most effective weight-management strategies known. The procedure requires approximately one hour, during which there are no distractions.

HAND LEVITATION TECHNIQUE

> Assume a comfortable, seated position. With your hands resting on your thighs, palm sides down, take several deep breaths, exhaling slowly. Imagine your

lungs soaking in pure, fresh energy, revitalizing your body's organs, and washing away all the impurities in your physical systems. Affirm your intent to enter hypnosis, then with your eyes closed, concentrate your full attention on your hands. As you picture your hands, notice every sensation, specifically the weight of your hands, along with any tingling, numbness, warmth or coolness, moisture in your palms, and looseness in the joints of your fingers. Now focus your full attention on *either* hand, and notice the sensation in that hand, paying particular attention to impressions of heaviness. Next, suggest to yourself that the heaviness in your hand is being replaced by sensations of weightlessness. At this point, give your hand permission to float upward, rising gently toward your forehead, as if a balloon were tied around your wrist, or as if a current of air were pushing the hand upward. As your hand moves upward, give yourself permission to enter hypnosis as soon as your hand touches your forehead. Allow plenty of time for your hand to reach your forehead, then allow it to return gently to its original position as you affirm:

> *I am now going deeper and deeper into hypnosis. I am comfortable and secure, at peace with myself and the world. As I now picture a serene lake and a white sail drifting gently in the breeze, I am becoming increasingly relaxed. All my cares are far, far away. On the distant side of the lake, green trees of many shades are silhouetted against a clear, peaceful sky. Overhead, a fluffy cloud drifts gently against the clear blue sky. As I continue picturing this relaxing scene, I am going*

deeper and deeper into hypnosis. I am now absorbing peaceful tranquillity deep into my innermost being.

By now counting backwards from five to one, I will drift even deeper into hypnosis. Upon the count of one, I will be ready to respond to each of my affirmations. Five—deeper and deeper; four—comfortable and relaxed, three—at complete peace; two—very, very deep; and finally, one.

As I remain in deep hypnosis, I am drifting gently into the future, slowly moving forward in time. Now in the future, I see myself standing before a full-length mirror, and weighing exactly (here, state your desired weight). *Surrounding my body is a radiant, glowing aura of health and vitality.* (Pause at this point to allow vivid imagery to unfold. Note specifically the glow of energy enveloping your body.) *As I focus on this image and its vibrant aura of color, my total being is infused with healthy, beaming energy. This is the true me—healthy, attractive, confident, and secure. Day by day, I am becoming the total person that I now view in the mirror. This is my goal, to weigh the amount that is good for me, to be healthier, and to enjoy life more. I will achieve this goal. Each day, I will eat only the right foods in the right amounts. I will eat sensibly and slowly, and I will enjoy each morsel to its fullest. Each day of progress will empower me with future success. I will become healthier and more self-assured. I am in charge of my body and my health destiny. All*

Hand Levitation Technique

my inner resources are now at my command. I will use them as needed to empower myself with health and success. I will discover new ways of enjoying my life to its fullest.

In the future, when I picture the colorful aura of vibrant energy surrounding me, I will be instantly empowered with vitality, motivation, and determination. By imaging this radiant glow, I will activate my subconscious powers and infuse my total being with healthy energy and success potential.

I am now ready to return to the present, bringing with me all the power I need to enrich my life with success. (Facilitate your return to the present by focusing attention on your body and its sensations.)

I am now in the present, and fully aware of my surroundings. I will exit hypnosis by slowly counting from one to five. On the count of five, I will be totally alert, refreshed, and empowered. Each suggestion I have given myself during this trance will remain deep within my being, growing stronger and stronger, day by day. One—becoming more alert; two—feeling alert and refreshed; three—more and more alert; four—fully alert and completely refreshed; and five—totally empowered and fully awake.

This procedure can be practiced daily or as frequently as desired to reinforce its empowering effects. Envisioning the body's surrounding aura of colorful energy at any time instantly activates the inner resources required for successful weight control. Although this procedure is specifically designed for weight management, other benefits such as increased motivation, self-confidence, and well-being, are invariably among its by-products.

SMOKING CESSATION

Perhaps the most effective induction procedure for breaking the smoking habit is the "Finger Spread Technique." This strategy sets the stage for procedures designed to strengthen the will to stop smoking, and call forth supportive subconscious forces to ensure success. The physical and psychological needs to smoke are addressed and extinguished. One session is usually enough to bring about an immediate cessation of smoking.

The induction procedure involves intentionally tensing the fingers of either hand, and counting backwards as the fingers are slowly relaxed. The trance state is deepened by inducing, then removing, sensations of dullness in the fingers. In self-hypnosis, removing a sensation is typically simpler and more deepening than inducing the sensation. The habit-control affirmations, along with an empowering post-hypnotic cue, are presented only after a trance of sufficient depth has been achieved.

FINGER SPREAD TECHNIQUE

Assume a comfortable, seated or reclining position, then slow your breathing, taking a little longer to exhale. While continuing to breathe slowly and rhythmically, close your eyes, and relax your body, progressively, from your head downward. Affirm your intent to enter hypnosis. With your hands resting on your thighs, spread the fingers of either hand, and hold the tense, spread position. As you notice the tension in your fingers and hand spreading upward into your arm and shoulder, affirm:

> As I prepare to enter hypnosis, I am surrounded by peace and tranquillity. I am calm and secure—at complete peace with myself and the universe. As I slowly count backwards from ten, my hand will become increasingly relaxed. I will become more and more comfortable, as each number takes me deeper and deeper into hypnosis. Upon the count

Finger Spread Technique

of one, my hand will be fully relaxed, and I will be in a deep, trance state. Ten—my fingers are beginning to slowly relax; nine—I am comfortable and secure as my fingers continue to relax; eight—relaxation is slowly spreading into my hand and upward into my arm; seven—relaxation is now spreading over my total body; six—I am becoming more and more comfortable, more and more relaxed; five—comfortable and secure; four—very, very relaxed; three—deeper and deeper, very, very deep; two—deeper and deeper into hypnosis; and finally, one.

My hand is now loose and limp, and my body is fully relaxed. I am now ready to go even deeper into hypnosis, as I again focus on my hand, paying attention to every sensation—tingling here and there, warmth in my palms, and pressure sensations at my fingertips. As I focus on my little finger, the sensations are now giving way to dullness. (Here, allow sufficient time for the dullness to occur.) *Now, the dullness in my little finger is spreading into the finger next to it. Both fingers are becoming duller and duller.* (As before, allow sufficient time for the dullness to occur.) *The dullness in my little finger and the finger next to it is now spreading over my entire hand. My hand is becoming duller and duller. All other feeling is now gone from my hand; only dullness remains.* (Allow the dullness to continue for a few moments before removing it.) *The dullness is now leaving as other feelings— warmth, tingling, pressure—return to my hand. My hand is now normal in every respect. I can now signal to myself that the dullness is gone by simply lifting my little finger.* (Pause here as you lift your little finger, then return it to its relaxed position.) *I am now ready to respond to each of my affirmations.*

I am determined to break the cigarette habit. I have all the resources I need to achieve this goal. I now assume complete control over this habit. All my

*inner resources—conscious and subconscious—
are poised to empower me with determination and
success. I possess an abundance of psychic
resources, with power to break the chains of this
habit, and to extinguish any desire to smoke. All of
my inner powers are now working with me to
empower me with mastery and complete success. I
now free myself, once and for all, of this habit, and
the health threats associated with it.*

*Beginning now, I will smoke no more. I am now a
non-smoker. By simply spreading my fingers,
then slowly relaxing them while affirming, "I am
a non-smoker," I can call forth an abundance of
inner resources to ensure my continued success,
day in and day out. Empowered with success, I
can now focus on other important goals in my life.*

*I am now ready to come out of this trance state
by counting from one to five. With each number,
I will become more and more awake and
refreshed. Upon the count of one, I will be fully
awake and alert. The affirmations I have presented to myself will remain deep within my
being to empower me with complete success.
One—becoming more alert; two—feeling
refreshed; three—more alert; four—fully awake
and empowered; and finally, five.*

This procedure illustrates the effectiveness of positive affirmation
to extinguish an undesired behavior with both mental and physical
components. Each affirmation is presented convincingly, in a positive, factual manner. With this procedure, the anticipation of success
is a given; the prospect of failure is inconceivable.

The Finger Spread Technique has been effectively adapted to a variety of other goals, particularly athletic proficiency. The smoking-related content of the procedure is replaced by suggestions related to activities such as accelerating development of specific athletic skills, building team spirit, or improving competitive performance. When practiced immediately prior to a competitive event, this versatile technique has demonstrated remarkable effectiveness in strengthening motivation and increasing accuracy. In team events, such as basketball, hockey, and football, it has been used to maximize team coordination and build endurance. In tennis, golf, and archery, the technique has been highly effective in promoting the overall quality of performance, and in overcoming mental blocks.

PAIN MANAGEMENT

Reducing or alleviating pain is often a side-benefit of self-hypnosis, particularly from procedures inducing relaxation and a tranquil, serene state of mind. The total alleviation of physical pain is not always desired, however, because a degree of pain can provide valuable information during treatment. Two pain-management strategies are specifically designed to either reduce or alleviate physical pain, while promoting wellness. The "Therapeutic Exchange Procedure," a somewhat passive, yet positive strategy, replaces pain with soothing relaxation. The "Pain Confrontation Procedure," while also positive, assertively confronts pain and extinguishes it. The Therapeutic Exchange Procedure is particularly useful in reducing physical pain with apparently no related psychological factors. The Pain Confrontation Procedure, on the other hand, is highly effective for reducing pain of psychological origin, as well as pain related to various medical conditions with contributing psychological factors.

Both strategies reject ownership of pain. Pain is addressed as "the pain," or "the discomfort," not as "my pain" or "my discomfort."

The "Peripheral Glow Technique" is the preferred trance-induction method for both pain-management strategies. The technique uses a stationary, glowing or shiny object, such as a candle or quartz crystal, positioned at or slightly above eye level, for induction in an upright, seated position. If a reclining position is preferred, a shiny tack positioned on the ceiling, to facilitate a slight upward gaze, is usually effective.

PERIPHERAL GLOW TECHNIQUE

> Assume a comfortable position, and concentrate for a few moments on your breathing. After affirming your intent to enter hypnosis, take several deep breaths, and develop a slow, rhythmic, breathing pattern. Mentally scan your body from your head downward, and allow areas of tension to fully relax. Take plenty of time to relax your total body, then focus your full attention on the shiny object. Gradually expand your peripheral vision to the area immediately surrounding the object, while still focusing on the object itself. Continue to expand your peripheral vision, slowly taking in more and more of the area around the object until you reach your peripheral limits, with your eyes still fixed on the object. Next, allow your vision to shift slightly out of focus, whereupon you will immediately notice a whitish glow emanating from the object, and permeating its surroundings. Slowly close your eyes, and notice the deep relaxation spreading over your face and throughout your body. Allow yourself to enter the trance state by slowly counting backwards from ten, as

relaxation soaks deeper and deeper into your muscles and joints. As the trance ensues, allow yourself to go deeper into hypnosis, using such techniques as peaceful imagery and additional reverse counting, until you reach the desired trance level.

For the THERAPEUTIC EXCHANGE PROCEDURE, the trance state is maintained at a moderate level as the following affirmations are presented:

> I am now absorbing soothing relaxation throughout my body. Relaxation is now gently flowing into the area of physical pain. Slowly, the pain is giving way to warm, soothing relaxation. The tissue and fiber surrounding the area of discomfort are now loose and engulfed with relaxation. Soothing relaxation is now gently easing away the pain.
>
> As I picture myself in my favorite place, I am becoming more comfortable, at complete peace. (Here, allow adequate time to form relaxing images of your favorite place, while slowly breathing in relaxation.) All my fears and anxieties are dissolving as my body becomes infused with pure, healing energy. I am now liberated from invading pain. I am protected, confident, and secure. I am now empowered to subdue pain and replace it with wellness and relaxation. My inner powers are working with me as I work with them.
>
> I am enveloped by a protective, luminous shield of health and vitality. Each day, the shield of healthful energy will become more and more powerful. I will be in complete command of any

future invasion of pain by first envisioning the luminous shield surrounding my body, then slowly breathing in relaxation, and finally, affirming, "I am empowered."

At this point, the trance is ended by slowly counting from one to five, while suggesting alertness and full wakefulness.

The second pain management option, PAIN CONFRONTATION PROCEDURE, which also requires a moderate trance state, is implemented as follows:

I will no longer be victimized by pain. I now disown it and steadfastly renounce it. As I approach the region of invading pain, I am fully confident of my power to eliminate it completely. I now confront it, experiencing it in its fullest intensity, and absorbing it totally. I no longer fear pain, because I am now in charge of it. I now banish it from my body, as I replace it with radiant, healing energy.

My life is now empowered with confidence, security, well-being, and freedom to achieve my highest levels of success and fulfillment. Because I have mastered pain and its consequences, I can now focus on other important goals. I will defeat any future invasion of pain by simply affirming, "I am empowered."

The trance is here ended by first reaffirming the enduring, empowering effects of the trance, then counting slowly from one to five, while presenting suggestions of being alert and awake.

Both of these procedures can be expanded to include additional post-hypnotic cues to extinguish any future threat of pain. Effective cues are joining the tips of the fingers, lifting a toe, stroking the ear lobe, and recalling a designated word or image.

REJUVENATION AND WELLNESS

The subconscious is a powerhouse of rejuvenation and wellness. The potential to be healthier, stay younger, and live longer exists in everyone. Self-hypnosis can empower us to tap into that potential, and generate an interaction that infuses our mental and physical systems with positive, youthful energy.

Through a procedure called "Star Gaze," the mind and body are saturated with rejuvenating energy, awakening dormant potentials and bathing organs and systems with health and vitality. The Star Gaze procedure stimulates inner-growth factors to form new, rejuvenating connections in the central nervous system. Mental and physical aging is slowed, arrested, or even reversed, as vitality and wellness are unleashed. Regardless of age or health status, frequent practice of this procedure can result in a healthier, younger body, and a happier, longer life. Star Gaze is essentially a progressive imagery model of trance induction.

STAR GAZE PROCEDURE

Allow approximately thirty minutes, with no distractions, for the procedure.

Step 1 Assume a comfortable, reclining position and, with your eyes closed, envision a dark sky with a single star. Take plenty of time for the star to appear in bright, bold contrast to the dark sky. Once the star is visible, focus only on the star for a few moments, then envision four brilliant surrounding stars, all equally spaced around the central star. Continue focusing on the central star for several moments as you become increasingly relaxed.

Step 2   Beginning with one of the four surrounding stars, shift your focus clockwise from star to star, slowly counting the stars as you go: one, two, three, and four. Repeat this procedure, resting your gaze for a few moments on each of the four stars, while suggesting to yourself that you are becoming increasingly relaxed and responsive to your affirmations.

Step 3   Concentrate on the central star while expanding your peripheral vision to take in the four surrounding stars. Notice other stars of varying brilliance and color beginning to appear. Soon the sky is filled with a magnificent display of stars. Some appear alone and isolated, whereas others form glowing clusters or brilliant ribbons across the sky. Some gather to form intricate patterns and dazzling, geometric designs. Some appear nearby and pulsate with power; others are barely visible in the distant reaches of the universe.

Step 4   After scanning the star-studded heavens for a few moments, return to the star where you began. Note that it is now the brightest star in the sky. Continue gazing at the star as you affirm:

> *This is my personal star. It belongs to me. It is my contact with the universe. It symbolizes the unlimited potential within myself, and my capacity to*

reach beyond the borders of my present existence to experience the vastness of the universe. As I gaze at this star, I am becoming increasingly aware of the spark of divine power within myself. My innermost being is now pulsating with power. I am now empowered to achieve my loftiest goals, and to realize my highest potentials. The spark of light within myself is now a glowing, pulsating, rejuvenating force, infusing my body with youthful vigor and wellness.

Step 5   Imagine the powerful, glowing light form at the solar plexus center of your body, reaching forth as a ray of light to connect you to your star in the heavens. Give your star a name—any name that comes to mind—and reaffirm that the powerful star belongs to you. As you remain connected to the star as a power source, draw energy from it and affirm:

> *The energies of youth and health are now permeating my body.*

Then imagine your body enveloped in a pulsating, rejuvenating glow, as you remain connected to your personal star. Focus on the inner core of glowing energy, and release your inner capacity for youth and wellness. Let sparkling, abounding energy flood your body with the glow of youth and wellness. Remind yourself that you are intimately connected to the illimitable power of the universe, and that your affirmations are promises of future realities.

Step 6   Focus on specific physical systems or organs and energize them with healing, rejuvenating power. As you remain connected to your personal star, present the following post-hypnotic affirmation:

Envisioning my personal star or calling its name at any time and under any circumstance will be instantly empowering to me.

Step 7 End the procedure by suggesting:

As I count from one to five, I will become increasingly alert. On the count of five, I will be fully awake. One, two, three, four, and five.

Following practice of this procedure, simply envisioning the star, or calling it by name, will instantly activate and magnify the empowering effects of this strategy. Although this exercise may seem primarily meditative in nature, it is designed to induce an empowered trance state, in which responsiveness to suggestion is heightened, and the inner and outer sources of power are accessed and maximized.

These are just a few examples of the use of hypnosis to promote health and fitness. Self-hypnosis is a flexible tool. Numerous other trance-induction procedures have been developed, and can be tailored to meet a variety of personal empowerment goals. Many subjects of self-hypnosis find that practice and experience with various induction and management procedures is required to maximize the empowering possibilities of this useful tool. One of the most advanced induction procedures is "Induction by Intent." This skill is typically acquired through extensive practice and mastery of other step-by-step induction techniques. Induction by Intent requires only seconds to implement, and consists of settling back, clearing the mind, and affirming, *I now give myself permission to enter the trance state.* When a sufficient depth has been achieved, usually within seconds, selected goal-related imagery and affirmations are presented. For this advanced approach, the trance is typically ended by simply deciding to come out of hypnosis.

Another highly useful induction technique is the "Upward Gaze," a rapid induction procedure, easily mastered by most subjects. To implement this procedure, assume a comfortable, relaxed position, and affirm your intent to enter hypnosis. Then, with your eyes open, shift your gaze to its uppermost position, without tilting your head backward. While holding the upward gaze, slowly close your eyes. Once your eyes are closed, allow them to return to their normal position, then apply selected deepening procedures, such as reverse counting and suggestions of drowsiness and relaxation.

A final procedure, the "Aura Hand Viewing Technique," discussed in the next chapter, can readily be adapted for use as a self-hypnosis tool. Although originally designed as an aura-viewing strategy, it is particularly useful for induction in programs formulated to increase awareness of higher planes of power.

Through self-hypnosis, we can discover many exciting new sources of power and ways of tapping into them. The result is an enriched, more fully empowered life, filled with health, success, happiness, and challenge.

❦ 3 ❦

THE HUMAN AURA:
ENERGIES OF BEING

The human aura is one of the major components in the body's complex energy system. Under appropriate viewing conditions, the aura appears as a colorful glow, actively enveloping the physical body, and extending in all directions to distances ranging from a few inches to several feet. Each aura is unique and relatively stable. Although continuous change characterizes the aura's color and energy patterns, the fundamental structure of each aura, sometimes called the "aura signature," remains essentially unchanged.

The basic nature of the aura, including its physical characteristics and psychic significance, has been the subject of wide speculation. One theory says that the aura is a purely biological phenomenon—a physical extension of our biological make-up. A related view holds that the human aura is essentially electromagnetic in nature, and little different from the electromagnetic field surrounding all living things. According to these views, the human aura would hold limited psychical or psychological significance, and little relevance to health and fitness.

Some experts, however, assert that the human aura is an integral part of our total being. As a dynamic combination of a universal life force and personal consciousness, the aura is seen as a reflection of our non-biological double, sometimes called the "astral body." From this perspective, the aura represents our spiritual part—the essence of our conscious being. It provides a summation of our existence, including past experiences, present interactions, and future growth potential. If properly understood, the aura could offer a detailed chronicle of our past and a reliable forecast of our future. As a manifestation of our inner life force, it embodies the eternal energies of life and existence itself. This view is supported by the fact that, at death, a glowing, aura-like form is often seen hovering briefly over the physical body, then slowly ascending; and following death, the physical body is no longer enveloped in the aura.

The psychic-empowerment model of health and fitness integrates aspects of each of these positions into a framework which recognizes the biological, environmental, psychological, and psychical dimensions of the aura system. We are essentially an energy system—mentally, physically, and spiritually—with the capacity to interact with other systems by generating, sending, and receiving energy. Our personal energy system, with its unique inner core, is a perpetual, energizing force which can engage the outermost planes of the universe. A major part of that energy system is its external component—the human aura.

The biological system provides a physical structure within which the aura, and its essential components, exist and function. Although biological processes interact with the aura, the aura system is neither dependent upon, nor limited to, the existence of a biological structure. Nevertheless, interacting biological factors can assert a visible influence. Among the critical conditions affecting the aura are dysfunctions among organs or any disruption in a biological system. In the visible aura, these effects can take numerous forms, including turbulence, contraction, discoloration, and even structural change.

In addition to biological components, a host of psychological and social factors act to influence the aura. Included are external stimulants, pressures, and stressors, along with attracting and repelling influences, including the aural energies of other individuals. A positive mood state, high self-esteem, and rewarding interactions with others who have achieved a high level of psychic actualization, are among the empowering conditions which strengthen the aura and replenish its energy supply. Stressful interactions, a poor self-concept, and negative emotional states such as hostility, frustration, and resentment, are among the conditions which deplete and weaken the aura. Typically, factors which promote our personal well-being are also conducive to a healthy aura.

Each aura emits frequencies which provide a useful index of personal growth and development. These frequencies, sometimes called the "pulse of the soul," can be sensed through a technique called the "Aura Caress." By simply allowing the wrist to rest lightly in the palm of the hand, we can sense unique aura patterns and characteristics, such as vibrations, balance, harmony, intensity, and resonance. With practice, we can use this technique to gauge the developmental level of our own aura, as well as those of others.

The aura's frequency patterns exist on a seven-point scale, with one representing the lowest level of personal unfoldment, but not necessarily an absence of growth potential. At seven, the highest and most forceful level, the frequencies are a symphony of perfection. Needless to say, few individuals on this earth plane attain level seven. The average frequency pattern is around level three or four. As we develop both mentally and spiritually, the aura also develops, and its frequencies change accordingly. The aura frequencies of great humanitarians and gifted psychics are often found at very high levels on the seven-point scale.

The Aura Caress

The frequency characteristics of the aura are influenced by a variety of health and fitness factors. These factors do not alter the frequency level, but they can markedly affect its features. A disruption in aura pulsation, an anomaly known as "aura static," often reflects a disorder involving the central nervous system. A depressed mood state and chronic fatigue, along with respiratory problems, tend to weaken the vibrations. Emphysema is particularly damaging to the aura. Excessive stress and negative emotions have a disquieting effect, and almost always introduce discord into the frequency patterns. Bodily injuries produce localized effects in the aura at the area of injury. Although the effects of physical injury on the aura vary, they typically include turbulence in the aura's frequencies, a pattern which is particularly evident for serious injuries.

Apart from its frequency attributes, the aura system is characterized by reasonably stable color features. These features, which can span the color spectrum, provide a useful index into the personal characteristics of the individual. Individual observations of the aura often reveal an extensive range of colors in a rainbow pattern. A dominant color, however, is almost always apparent. Among the dominant colors most frequently observed in the aura are shades of blue, yellow, and green. Bright yellow is associated with high intelligence and sociability, although the two characteristics do not always exist together. Dull yellow is associated with stressful conditions asserting a negative influence on social interactions or intellectual efficiency. Bright green usually signals interest in the health professions or the presence of healing attributes. As expected, bright green is almost invariably dominant in the auras of health providers and gifted healers. Dull green in the aura is associated with low self-esteem, frustration, and envy. (The term, "green with envy," may have arisen from our subconscious perceptions of this color in the aura.) Bright blue represents tranquillity, cheerfulness, and optimism; whereas dull blue is often associated with despondency and a pessimistic outlook. "Feeling blue" may have a literal basis in the aura system.

Orange, as a dominant color in the aura, represents assertiveness, extroversion, and persuasive skills. This color is often dominant in the auras of attorneys and entrepreneurs. Pink is associated with artistic skills, cultural interests, sensitivity, and idealism. Although pink is found more often in the auras of women, educated men who are highly successful in their professions will frequently have areas of pink in their auras. Brown represents outdoor interests, mechanical skills, and strong independence. Noted with greater frequency in the auras of men, brown is often dominant in the auras of archaeologists, engineers, and mechanics. Purple suggests abstract interests and spiritual concerns: and not surprisingly, is often dominant in the auras of religious leaders, philanthropists, and philosophers. Areas of red, while usually transient, represent intense emotions such as passion and anger. Gray, in the aura, is a foreboding, but typically transient color, often foreshadowing illness or impending misfortune.

Certain conditions are known to have empowering effects on the aura, often depending upon the aura's color. For instance, intellectually challenging situations are particularly revitalizing to the dominantly yellow aura, whereas involvement in humanitarian efforts is characteristically energizing to the dominantly purple aura. Recreational activities, meditation, relaxing music, and interactions with nature are typically energizing to auras of any color or characteristic.

The aura is particularly sensitive to chemical substances. Alcohol, while temporarily "lighting up" the aura, constricts and depletes its energy. Nicotine and caffeine likewise constrict and deplete the aura, while introducing dinginess and drab discolorations. Drug dependence invariably discolors and enfeebles the aura. A dull, lifeless gray often characterizes the aura of long-term drug abusers.

Among the most critical factors influencing the aura are the aura systems of other individuals and groups with whom we interact. Our social relationships involve energy exchanges with either empowering or disempowering effects on the aura. Positive social interactions are almost always mutually energizing and empowering; however, negative social interactions almost always disrupt the aura's energy system.

Some aura systems tend to drain energy from other systems, a phenomenon known as "psychic vampirism." Because of their failure to develop their own aura systems, these "aura vampires," as they might be called, tend to tap into and feed upon the aura energies of others. They often include, but are not limited to, the pseudo intellectual, the religious fundamentalist, the identity-diffused, and the self-styled "debunkers" of psychic phenomena.

Aura vampires tend to be psychically immature, negatively focused, and rigid in their views of themselves and the world. They have neglected their own psychic growth and blocked their own energy systems. Consequently, they either intentionally or unintentionally lock their energy systems into those of surrounding individuals or even groups. The energy depletion occurs when the victim is in close proximity, but not necessarily in physical contact with the vampire. The result for the vampire is an immediate, but temporary, power surge. The unfortunate results for the incognizant victim are a depletion of energy, fatigue, and, in instances of prolonged depletion, even illness.

FINGER INTERLOCK

Aura vampirism can occur without the knowledge of either the vampire or the victim. Fortunately for the victim, the disempowering process, once it is known, can be prevented, or, if already in progress, terminated through a simple procedure called "Finger Interlock." This procedure, requiring only seconds to implement, is executed by joining the tips of the thumb and middle finger of each hand, then bringing them together to form interlocking circles, while mentally enveloping the body in a shield of positive energy. Finger Interlock is also useful as an instant relaxation technique, and is an effective strategy for heightening one's powers of influence and control. Frequent use of this technique tends to increase its empowering efficacy.

Despite the potentially disempowering effects of certain conditions and interactions, the healthy aura is usually self-sustaining. It is supported by its own internal energy source, and has the capacity to engage in constructive, empowering exchanges with other energy systems. The aura's health and wellness energies can promote one's own health and well-being, or they can be deliberately dispensed to benefit others. Physical health and wellness involving the purposeful transfer of positive energy is essentially a function of the aura's capacity to generate energy and send it, even from a spatial distance, typically through imagery and affirmation.

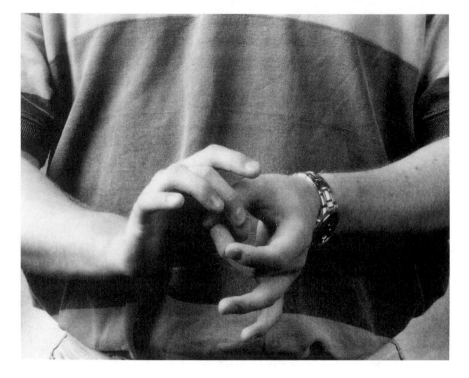

Finger Interlock

Exercising the aura's positive sending functions is consistently empowering to the sender and receiver alike. Conversely, any attempt to send negative energy, if only in the form of negative thought, is disempowering, but to the sender alone. Our negative thoughts and energies, like negative actions, close down our sending powers, while weakening the aura and depleting its energy supply. Fortunately, appropriate positive intervention empowers the aura to combat negative forces, and to extinguish all disempowering residue.

VIEWING THE AURA

Many of the health and fitness strategies associated with the aura require its actual viewing. Aside from facilitating aura intervention efforts, skill in viewing the aura can promote positive relationships and greater understanding of others, in wide ranging areas of human interaction. Counselors, teachers, therapists, and physicians, among other health and human-resource specialists, could appreciably enhance their effectiveness in working with others by recognizing the aura's relevance to our physical and mental well-being, and by developing aura-viewing skills.

Numerous procedures exist for viewing the aura. Although most of them were designed for use in viewing the auras of other persons, certain techniques are available for viewing one's own aura. One of the most highly effective self-viewing procedures is the "Aura Hand Viewing Technique." A single practice trial, using this technique, is usually sufficient to bring the aura into view.

AURA HAND VIEWING TECHNIQUE

> The hand is held at arm's length, against a white or off-white background screen, which can be situated a few inches to several feet away. The eyes are focused on the hand for a few moments, then peripheral vision is gradually expanded, taking in as much of the surroundings as possible. The aura will appear around the hand as a glow of energy, usually white at first, then in color. The colors and radiance of the aura around the hand are typically representative of the full aura.
>
> The Aura Hand Viewing Technique can be adapted for use as a powerful, hypnotic self-induction procedure. For this purpose, a seated position is required while focusing on the extended hand and, indirectly, on the energies surrounding it. The following affirmation is presented:

Aura Hand Viewing Technique

*The energies enveloping my hand and my total
being are now available to me, empowering me
to achieve my goal of (specify goal).*

Following suggestions of heaviness, the hand is allowed
to slowly return to a resting position. The eyes are then
closed, and selected procedures, such as relaxing
imagery and reverse counting, are applied to deepen
the trance to the desired level, at which appropriate
goal-related affirmations are presented.

This procedure is particularly effective for expanding inner
awareness, while opening the higher dimensions of power. As a
footnote, efforts to view one's aura in a mirror are usually unsuccessful, since mirrors do not appear to adequately reflect aura energies. The aura image seeming, at times, to appear in the mirror, is
more likely to be a visual illusion, not a reflection of the aura.

The best condition for viewing the aura of other persons is a quiet setting with either natural daylight or soft, indirect lighting. Although various mechanical aids to facilitate viewing the aura are commercially available, they are usually unnecessary, and can, in some instances, distort vision, making accurate viewing of the aura more difficult. A white or off-white, non-glossy screen, placed approximately two feet behind the subject being viewed, with the viewer situated at a distance of at least ten feet from the subject, is sufficient for practice viewing. Almost anyone can succeed in viewing the aura and its colors under appropriately controlled viewing conditions with practice. Once developed, aura-viewing skills are easily transferred to a wide range of real-life circumstances, including by moonlight—a method preferred by some experienced viewers.

Two procedures are recommended for viewing the aura of another person: the "Focal Shift Technique" and the "Focal Point Technique." A single attempt using either of these strategies, results in success for most people. Although the Focal Shift Technique is somewhat easier for most viewers, the Focal Point Technique is particularly effective for viewers who experience difficulty perceiving color in the aura.

FOCAL SHIFT TECHNIQUE

Step 1 While in a mentally passive, relaxed state, select a point of focus on the subject's forehead or shoulder, and gaze at that point.

Step 2 Continue to focus your full attention on the selected point, then gradually expand your peripheral vision in all directions—left and right, above and below the subject—until you reach your limits for peripheral vision.

Step 3 Allow your eyes to shift slightly out of focus. You will immediately notice a white glow around the subject's

body. Gradually, the white glow (essentially a perceptual illusion) will be replaced by the visible aura,
which is usually seen as color and movement surrounding the body.

Step 4   View specific areas and characteristics of the aura, paying particular attention to colors, energy patterns, and
unique features.

The Focal Point Technique uses a small, shiny object—typically a
gold or silver dot or star—affixed to the background viewing screen
as a focal point. For best results, the object is positioned a few inches directly overhead, or to the upper left or right side of the subject.

FOCAL POINT TECHNIQUE

Step 1   With your eyes closed, take a few deep breaths as you
relax your body and clear your mind of active thought.

Step 2   Following a few moments of relaxation, focus your
eyes on the shiny object behind the subject.

Step 3   Continue to focus on the object until a whitish glow
appears around the subject, usually within a few seconds. As your eyes remain focused on the object, allow
a few moments for color to appear in the aura.

Step 4   Shift your focus from the shiny object to the aura
itself, with its variations of color, motion, and other
characteristics.

With the aura in view, using either of these techniques, problem
areas, such as discolorations, breaks, depressions, and imbalances,
become visible and subject to healthful intervention.

AURA HEALTH AND FITNESS STRATEGIES

Several excellent aura-intervention strategies have been specifically formulated to empower one's personal aura system, and the aura systems of others, with abundant, healthy energy. No human system is more critical to our physical and mental well-being than the aura, which is in constant interaction with the physical body. Empowering strategies applied to others will involve some form of energy interaction or transfer. Consequently, empowering one's own aura system is an essential prerequisite to empowering the aura systems of others.

A four-step procedure, designed to generate positive aura energies, and initiate a healing and wellness interaction between the aura and the physical body, is the "Aura Health and Wellness Interaction Procedure." The procedure can be used to empower oneself and, if desired, to send positive energy to a distant recipient.

Aura Health and Wellness Interaction Procedure

Step 1   With your eyes closed, settle back and mentally scan your body, pausing at points of stress and tension. Deliberately release the tension and infuse your whole body with relaxation. Allow plenty of time to become fully relaxed, then affirm,

> *I am comfortable, relaxed, and secure.*

Step 2   Form images of a glowing blanket of bright energy at your feet, slowly rising to envelop your body. Allow time for the blanket to enfold you, then affirm:

> *I am infused with positive, powerful energy. I am surrounded by the invigorating energies of good health and wellness.*

Step 3   Focus on the receiving target. If the target is yourself, form an image of your physical body, and allow the full body to soak in the surrounding energies of health and wellness. Bathe your body systems and organs in the glow of health and vitality. If your target recipient is another person, form a mental image of that individual, then release radiant, healing energies as a glowing form to envelop the full body of the recipient. Mentally stay with your recipient for a few moments, as the energies of health and wellness are being absorbed.

Step 4   Conclude by affirming:

> *I am now infused with positive aura energy and potential. I am empowered to use these resources to enrich my life and the lives of others.*

This procedure is followed by a brief period of introspection and reflection, during which the infusion process continues.

We can promote our physical and mental well-being by developing a strong, positive aura system. A highly effective self-empowering technique is the "Aura Intervention Procedure," which liberates submerged aura energies, replenishes the external aura, and generates a healthy, positive interaction between the aura system and the physical body.

Aura Intervention Procedure

Step 1   Settle back and let yourself become comfortable and relaxed. With your eyes closed, form an image of a powerful, internal, super energy core in the center of your body. Picture the core as a glowing inner vertical bar of positive energy.

Step 2 Mentally release powerful energy from the central energy core to radiate throughout your physical body. Flood your total body with positive, vitalizing, rejuvenating energy.

Step 3 Focus on particular organs and systems, bathing them in the glow of powerful energy. Allow plenty of time for your body to absorb this invigorating energy.

Step 4 Permit the energy emitted from the central energy core to extend beyond your body as a brilliant energy force, radiating in all directions.

Step 5 Conclude by affirming:

> *I am infused with abundant energy. I am enveloped in a radiant glow of health and vitality. My total being is revitalized and invigorated with positive energy. I am empowered.*

The Aura Intervention Procedure is not limited to health and fitness goals only; it can also be used to counteract negative forces such as fear, insecurity, and depression, which tend to disempower the aura. Actors and performers report that combinations of this procedure and the Finger Interlock technique are highly effective in intercepting fear, reducing stress, and improving their performance skills. Students have found these techniques useful in controlling anxiety, building self-confidence, and improving their test scores. Athletes have used these techniques to improve the quality of their performance in a wide range of skills requiring psychomotor coordination or physical prowess.

The "Aura Massage" is an empowerment technique designed to balance the aura, and unleash its blocked energies. This energizing procedure, which intervenes directly in the recipient's aura system, focuses on the positive interaction of aura energy fields. It employs both general and specific hand-massage techniques, applied a few inches away from the physical body, while carefully avoiding all physical touch. Any physical contact during the massage can interrupt the empowering process.

AURA MASSAGE

The massage procedure is initiated by instructing the recipient, who can be seated, standing, or reclining, to become mentally passive and physically relaxed, while breathing slowly and rhythmically. The general massage, a two-step procedure, begins with a gentle, circular stroking of the energies surrounding the recipient's head, and then slowly progresses downward, with continued circular motions, always avoiding any physical contact. Once this step is complete, the aura is again massaged, but with a series of downward strokes only. Each downward stroke is ended with a brisk outward motion, away from the body. As with the first step, the second step begins at the head, and progresses downward over the body.

Upon completion of the two-step general massage, the procedure specifically focuses on areas of aura weakness or dysfunction. Stressed areas are gently massaged with light, half-circular motions, to reduce tension. Areas of turbulence and imbalance are stroked in a series of long, downward movements, followed by slow, circular strokes, to generate a more harmonious flow of energy. Breaks in the aura, a condition associated with either physical or psychological trauma, are closed by applying several short, up-and-down and side-to-side strokes, followed by gentle strokes that spiral upward.

With experience, problem areas in the aura can be detected either visually or through aura touch.

The results of the aura massage are essentially the product of the interaction of the two aura systems. It would follow that the psychological and auric state of the masseur are critical to the effectiveness the procedure. The essential characteristics of the skilled masseur are an abundance of aura energy, a balanced, harmonious aura system, and a genuine regard for the massage recipient. Throughout the procedure, positive affirmations, focusing on desired effects, are formulated and presented either mentally or verbally.

Certain elements of the aura massage can be applied to oneself. In auto-massage, the essential conditions remain unchanged. The massage techniques can vary, but they are always accompanied by positive affirmations of desired results.

In addition to empowering the aura energy system, the aura massage is particularly useful as a pain-management strategy. For that purpose, relevant empowering affirmations, designed to control pain, are presented at frequent intervals throughout the procedure. Examples of effective affirmations are:

> *The discomfort in your body is now giving way to relaxation. You are becoming more and more comfortable, as the pain eases away. Your body is now enveloped in the abundant energies of health and wellness.*

The aura massage can also be used to promote a general state of wellness. The body's defense mechanisms and immune system seem particularly responsive to this technique. As in pain management, this application of the aura massage presents relevant affirmations during the procedure which can include the following:

The organs and systems of your body are infused
with powerful health and wellness energy. Your
body's defenses are fully energized, and your
immune system fully activated. Your total being
is revitalized with powerful energy.

ENERGY TRANSFER STRATEGY

The "Energy Transfer Strategy" is used to add energy to
the aura. It can be used independently, or in conjunc-
tion with the Aura Massage. The procedure is initiated
by vigorously rubbing the hands together to generate
energy, while images of a desired color are formed. The
use of color in this procedure is based on the significance of particular colors in the aura as previously discussed. As the hands are rubbed together, relevant
affirmations are formed to accompany the images of
color. The generated energy is then transferred to the
subject's aura through gentle circular motions. The procedure is concluded by focusing on any problem areas
and lightly massaging them with upward, spiraling
motions, as relevant affirmations are presented.

The Energy Transfer Strategy has been effectively used to reduce
pain, alleviate migraine and tension headaches, promote tissue
repair, and, in some reported instances, even improve hearing and
vision. These empowering effects, while based on somewhat sub-
jective reports and observations, suggest a remarkable potential for
intervention with the functions of physical organs and systems for
better health and fitness.

The spontaneous transfer of aura energy is probably a continuous, ongoing process. We have all experienced the energizing and

empowering effects of positive person-to-person or group interactions, in which empowering energies were sensed, perhaps physically as well as mentally. On the other hand, we also may have experienced the disempowering, and often fatiguing effects of negative interactions. In our social interactions, we typically back away from incompatible or repelling energy sources, in an effort to generate a comfortable distance, and to prevent, perhaps subconsciously, the transfer of negative energy. When the energy source is compatible or attracting, we often engage it by moving into the energy field, and welcoming the empowering exchange. In other words, we spontaneously back away from people or move toward them, depending upon the positive or negative interactions of our energy systems. These spatial movements have their counterparts in the human aura; negative energy interactions constrict the aura, whereas positive energy interactions expand it. Aura-viewing techniques can be used to reveal these reactions as they occur.

Incompatible or conflicting relationships are often reflected in the aura, a phenomenon sometimes seen in the counseling setting. In a partner-counseling situation, the aura of a woman whose partner had been unfaithful showed a constriction with a serious tear. When asked to draw how she felt, she drew a picture of a heart torn into two pieces. Her partner's aura was likewise constricted, with severe turbulence and discoloration. When asked to draw how he felt, he drew a picture of himself overshadowed by a dark, threatening cloud. As they resolved the problems in their relationship, their auras became increasingly bright and expansive.

Many of our spontaneous, aura interactions have important health and fitness implications. For instance, a mother whose teenage son suffered frequent epileptic seizures, noted that when her mood state was distressed, her son appeared to be more prone to seizures. The seizures appeared to be related to her anxiety regarding her son's tenuous academic situation, even though she did not share those concerns with her son. She concluded that her own system generated and dispersed energies consistent with her mental state, and that these energies, in turn, physically affected her son. She began deliberately generating more positive thought energies, which included personal affirmations of self-worth and well-being. The results were an improved relationship with her son, and a marked decrease in the frequency of his seizures. Moreover, his academic performance dramatically improved.

The energies of the aura can exist in residual form beyond our immediate surroundings. This is particularly true of collective aura energies involving group gatherings. Group-generated energies, particularly when they are positive, literally permeate and charge the immediate physical surroundings. When the group is dispersed, its energies tend to linger in the physical setting. Many of us have experienced this phenomenon upon entering a room or auditorium recently occupied by a group. Although vacant, the setting remains charged by the energies generated and left behind by the group.

In our personal and psychic development, we grow through empowering experiences which become an integral part of our lives. The power to generate positive energies and disperse them is one of our most important resources. We can choose to empower our lives, and we can contribute to the empowerment of others. In the process, we give and receive, while contributing to the greater whole.

Individually and collectively, we can promote empowerment of the globe, by dispersing positive energies around the planet and throughout the universe. The limits of our aura systems are unknown. With the aura's central core of power intact, the energies of the aura could conceivably reach into infinity. Empowered with such a system, which is just possibly the seat of our consciousness, our only limits as human beings are those we ascribe to ourselves.

*₊ 4 *₊

OUT-OF-BODY EXPERIENCES: ASCENDING IN POWER

Out-of-body experiences (OBEs) are experiences of being spatially located separate from the physical body. Also known as astral projection or astral travel, OBEs are typically considered a function of the astral or extrabiological body. The OBE concept holds that our extrabiological part is empowered to disengage the physical body, and in that out-of-body state, to experience distant realities, independent of physiology. Adding weight to this view is the profound sense of freedom and separateness from the physical which usually accompanies OBEs. In the out-of-body state, the astral disengagement is partial and transient, because the biological-astral connection, sometimes called the "silver cord," remains intact to energize and enliven the biological body. At death, the connecting cord of energy is severed, and biological functions cease. Astral separation from the physical body at that point, is complete and permanent.

Such a duality of our basic nature suggests many empowerment possibilities, including a host of health and fitness applications. In the out-of-body state, personal identity and consciousness remain intact. Complex mental processes continue, but often in liberated, enhanced form. Higher mental capacities, including problem-solving, creativity, and psychic functions, are particularly energized by the out-of-body state.

The same faculties which enable us to interact with the physical world remain active in the out-of-body state. Sight, hearing, taste, touch, and smell continue unimpaired, and may be heightened. In the astral state, the capacity to influence distant situations or events is often observed, a phenomenon we call "Astral PK." Given the capacity of OBEs to influence external conditions, we can logically assume the possibility of out-of-body intervention into the functions of the physical body with which the astral body is connected. Frequently, the out-of-body experience involves higher-plane phenomena, such as interactions with familiar personalities who have made the transition to the other side. One of the most profound implications of OBEs is the certainty of higher dimensions of reality, and continued consciousness after death, with intellect and identity intact.

The out-of-body state is critical to our psychic-empowerment model of health and fitness, because it can set the stage for potentially empowering interactions between our biological and non-biological systems. In the normal state of awareness, our thought and imagery processes continuously interact with our physical body, to produce commensurate changes in our mental and physical state. Not surprisingly then, deliberate intervention into the thought and imagery system can produce related changes in the physical body, depending upon the nature of the intervention. Even a minor change in mental processes can initiate significant physical alterations reaching far beyond the central nervous system. In fact, a chain reaction is often initiated by a single thought, with our thought influencing our mood state, and our mood state, in turn, influencing our physiology. By assuming command of our thought and imagery functions, we can deliberately alter our mood state, and indirectly intervene into our physiology. Of course, that process can have empowering, as well as disempowering, consequences. Positive, empowering thoughts and images produce a positive mood state, while promoting a healthy, empowered biological state. Conversely, negative, disempowering thoughts and images can intervene into both mood state and biological system, to activate an unhealthy, disempowered state. The out-of-body experience promotes a psychically charged, cognitive and emotional state, thus empowering us to by-pass this chain reaction, and intervene directly into our biological functions. The result can be healthy, empowered physical and mental well-being.

The out-of-body state provides the ideal condition for initiating health and fitness strategies to energize the physical body as it rests in a passive, receptive state. In the out-of-body state, consciousness, with all its powers, is liberated from physiology. The biological limitations, and their disrupting effects on our psychic efforts to promote health and fitness, are minimized. Physiological functions are reduced or at rest, while mental processes continue unimpeded or even in enhanced form. In that state, the power of consciousness to intervene into physical functions is at its peak.

When we enter the out-of-body state, we experience a potentially empowering liberation of consciousness from the physical body. Individuals who enter the out-of-body state for the first time often describe the experience as "profound," "magnificent," "illuminating," and "spiritually enlightening." While apart from the body, we can experience first-hand our spiritual being, and the unlimited possibilities of a fully-liberated free will. With mastery of this important potential, intent alone is sufficient to instantly travel great distances, expand awareness, and intervene into physical realities to bring forth desired change.

HEALTH AND FITNESS APPLICATIONS

The application of OBEs to health and fitness requires mastery of appropriate strategies designed to induce the empowered out-of-body state and, while maintaining that state, to engage the physical body in a healthy interaction. Out-of-body self-induction strategies are usually acquired easily, possibly because spontaneous OBEs are common to all of us. Losing track of time, certain so-called daydreams, various meditative states, and blanks in memory, are common spontaneous OBEs.

One view of OBEs holds that sleep is an out-of-body state, in that, as we fall asleep, our non-biological part disengages the biological body. In that suspended state, the astral body hovers closely over the physical body, or travels to great distances. Certain "lucid dream" experiences, particularly those in which we seem to drift over familiar terrain, are typically seen as out-of-body travels, rather than dreams. In view of this probability, and the power of sleep to activate OBEs, it is not surprising that among the most effective strategies for promoting out-of-body travel to distant destinations are those which utilize procedures related to sleep.

"Pre-sleep Intervention" is designed to intervene into the out-of-body experience, beginning in the drowsy state just prior to sleep. This procedure permits conscious participation in the spontaneous out-of-body process before sleep, and allows continued conscious control of the experience during sleep. Because the procedure taps into the sleep process, it is easily mastered, and can be applied to an almost unlimited range of personal-empowerment goals. The following procedure is specifically adapted to meet health and fitness needs.

PRE-SLEEP INTERVENTION PROCEDURE

Step 1 In the earliest stage of drowsiness, affirm:

> *I am surrounded by peace and tranquillity. The abundant powers of my innermost self are at my command. I can activate them to enrich and empower my life. I am attuned to the highest energies of the universe. I can draw from them to energize my life with health, success, and fulfillment. I am mentally and physically responsive to the positive powers, both within myself and around me. As I travel out-of-body to experience other realities, I will be fully protected and secure.*

Step 2 As drowsiness deepens, generate images of your physical body at rest. Envision your personal consciousness as a light-form, rising gently from your physical body and hovering over it. With consciousness enveloped in light, view your physical body from overhead, and envision it bathed in radiant energy. Surround your body with the glow of health.

Step 3 Focus your attention on your specific health and fitness goals. Envision biological organs and functions, then direct your powerful energies of consciousness as beams of light, to infuse them with health and wellness. Affirm:

> *My total being is empowered with positive energy. I am fully infused with the powerful energies of health and wellness.*

Step 4 Envision the light of your astral being reaching upward to engage the higher planes of light in the universe. You can facilitate this process by envisioning a brilliant sphere of universal energy, from which you can draw unlimited power. In astral form, you can engage that sphere, and channel its energy to your biological body through the silver cord.

Step 5 As your astral being remains spontaneously suspended over your physical body, affirm:

> *I am energized mentally, physically, and spiritually with the positive powers of my own being and the universe.*

Step 6 At this step, you may choose either to re-enter your physical body, or to continue the out-of-body experience, as drowsiness deepens and sleep ensues. At any point, you can re-engage your biological body by simply viewing it at rest, expressing your intent to re-enter your body, then focusing awareness on your breathing and selected physical sensations.

One of the most effective out-of-body self-induction procedures is called "Astral Trek." The procedure typically requires a period of approximately ten minutes for induction, and an additional thirty minutes for most health and fitness applications. Essential to the success of all out-of-body procedures is a safe setting, in which there are no distractions. As in self-hypnosis, any interruption during the procedure can negate potential empowerment benefits. A distraction during out-of-body travel can abort the experience, and complicate astral return to the physical body.

Astral Trek, like other OBE-induction procedures, requires conditions similar to those conducive to sleep. A comfortable, reclining or prone position is recommended, with legs uncrossed and hands resting at the sides. Lighting should be subdued.

ASTRAL TREK

Step 1 With your eyes closed, slow your breathing and relax your body. For this procedure, relaxation begins at the feet and culminates at the forehead. Mentally scan your body from your feet upward, forming a mental picture of your physical body at rest. Pause at stress points, and replace any build-up of tension with soothing relaxation. Upon reaching your forehead, mentally bathe your body in glowing energy, as you affirm:

> *I am safe, comfortable, and relaxed. As I prepare to leave my body, I am protected and secure. As I travel from my body, I will remain enveloped in a powerful shield of protection. Nothing can harm me as I travel out-of-body to experience other realities. I am empowered to return to my body with comfort and ease at any moment I decide to do so.*

Step 2 As relaxation deepens, form a mental picture of your body at rest. Notice the position of your body, and the details of your clothing. Envision yourself suspended above your body, looking down from above. Then, allow yourself to drift away from your body while remaining connected to it by a brilliant cord of glowing energy.

Step 3 Envision a peaceful scene, such as a familiar river, mountain range, or skyline at sunset. Absorb the peaceful tranquillity of the scene, then introduce motion into your imagery such as billowy clouds, floating balloons, ripples in water, or a slowly drifting boat.

Step 4 Envision yourself engaging a higher plane of radiant light. As you interact with that plane, allow the silver cord to become a channel for transporting healthy energy to your body at rest. While remaining suspended in space, affirm:

> *I am now out of my body. I am empowered and in full command of my faculties. I am attuned to the unlimited powers of the cosmos. I can now draw from the universe abundant power to energize my total being.*

As you continue to envision the silver cord as a powerful channel connecting you to your physical body, mentally infuse your body with healthy energy. Bathe specific organs, and energize particular bodily functions.

Step 5 To return to your physical body and end the OBE state, view your body from a distance and affirm:

> *I am now ready to return to my body.*

Gently allow yourself to descend as a light form merging with your physical body. Focus your attention on breathing and other physical sensations. Before opening your eyes, affirm:

> *I am now at one with my total being—physically, mentally, and spiritually. I am fully empowered in mind, body, and spirit.*

Step 6 The procedure is concluded by a brief period of reflection and reaffirmation of the empowering benefits of the experience.

PAIN MANAGEMENT

Among the most important health and wellness applications of the out-of-body state is pain management. During the OBE, pain is typically non-existent, and following a single session using OBE pain-management strategies, a significant reduction in pain often continues for several hours. Complete control over distressing, chronic pain is not unusual following a series of sessions and mastery of appropriate strategies. Many pain patients prefer out-of-body strategies over conventional pain-management programs, because it gives them a greater sense of control over their own body and the invasion of pain.

As with hypnosis, the complete removal of pain is not always the goal of OBE pain-management procedures. Some degree of pain or discomfort can provide important diagnostic information, as well as feedback on the effects of medical treatment. Pain, however, is often so severe that it causes harmful, debilitating effects. Under appropriate medical guidance, pain management through OBEs has three important goals—first, to extinguish pain totally when medically indicated; second, to reduce pain to moderate levels when total extinction is not recommended; and third, to promote wellness and a state of personal well-being.

One of the most effective out-of-body, pain-management procedures is called "Master of Pain." This strategy, which uses Astral Trek to induce the out-of-body state, is formulated not only to manage pain and advance wellness, but also to promote a sense of personal power and control over pain.

Master of Pain Procedure

Step 1   Induce the out-of-body state by implementing Steps One through Four of Astral Trek as previously presented.

Step 2   Upon completing Step Four of Astral Trek, and while remaining in the out-of-body state, affirm:

> *I am the master of pain.* (Note pain is referred to here as "pain," not "my pain.") *As master of pain, I am in control. I can reduce pain to dullness or discomfort and, when desired, extinguish it altogether. I will now bathe the sources of pain in positive, healing energy. My body, resting in peaceful serenity, is responsive to my touch, and the infusion of revitalizing energy.*

Upon completing these affirmations, view your body at rest, and focus on the locations of discomfort. Astrally zoom in on each affected area, and bathe it in glowing energy. Massage your total body with the glowing light of health and comfort, as you draw away the darkness of pain and tissue damage. Bathe the affected body parts, systems, and organs in radiant energy. Infuse the full body with the glow of health and vitality. As you work, give detailed attention to each physical aspect. Affirm:

> *This is my body. It is my temple. I respect it fully.*
> *I will care for it and guard it against harm.*

Step 3   Conclude the procedure by implementing Steps Five and Six of Astral Trek.

EMPOWERING THE IMMUNE SYSTEM

Empowering the body's immune system is one of the most promising applications of OBEs. Deficiencies in the immune system, including those caused by the human immunodeficiency virus (HIV), leave the body vulnerable to opportunistic infections and illnesses which would not be life-threatening in the absence of a disarmed immune system. The application of OBEs to empower the immune system is based on the two-fold premise that first, critical wellness mechanisms exist in the astral body, and second, the out-of-body state generates a responsive biological condition, permitting psychic intervention into the body's most complex systems.

The physical body is always subservient to the psychic mind. During the out-of-body state, the subdued physiology becomes increasingly receptive, providing the ideal state for psychic intervention. Out-of-body procedures involving the human immune system emphasize the capacity of the experience to generate empowering energy, and to focus it to alter physiology. As we experience the out-of-body state, our highest psychic potentials are activated and fully empowered to intervene into our physical systems. Malfunctioning immune programs can be unloaded, and functional programs installed. Any weakened or dormant system can be invigorated, and contaminated systems can be purified.

One of the most effective strategies designed to empower the immune system is the "Immune Empowerment Formula." Essentially an energy-purification process, this procedure arms the body's immune and defense systems with pure energy, while repelling invading, destructive forces, and initiating repair mechanisms.

IMMUNE EMPOWERMENT FORMULA

Step 1   Induce the out-of-body state using Steps One through Four of Astral Trek.

Step 2   Following Step Four of Astral Trek, view your physical body at rest, as you remain in the out-of-body state. Focus on your physical body's energy core at the solar plexus. Note the glowing astral cord, connecting you to this region and its core of pulsating energy.

Step 3   Allow the energies of your physical body to flow into the astral cord, and become absorbed into your astral body, but without fully depleting your biological body before it is again replenished. Carefully monitor this depleting and replenishing process by noting the glow around your physical body. As the glow diminishes, your body's energy is being depleted; as the glow expands, your body's energy is being replenished.

Step 4   Repeat the depleting-replenishing cycle until the glow around your physical body reaches its highest level of brilliance—usually accomplished within three cycles.

Step 5   Permit your astral and physical energies to become balanced by ending the cycling process and affirming:

> I am balanced mentally, physically, and spiritually. I am empowered with abundant health and wellness energy.

Step 6   Conclude the procedure by implementing Steps Five and Six of Astral Trek.

OBES AND HIGHER DIMENSIONS OF POWER

The out-of-body state provides the essential condition for accessing and interacting with the highest dimensions of health, power, and knowledge. The result can be a powerful infusion of healthy energy that fills our total being.

"OBEs Interdimensional Interaction" is based on the concept that beyond our known reality, many potentially empowering dimensions exist, and can be probed through the out-of-body experience. The procedure initiates astral travel and a dynamic out-of-body interaction with other dimensions of power. During that empowering interaction, the connecting silver cord becomes a dynamic vehicle for transporting abundant healing energy back to the biological body. Upon return and re-entry to the physical body, the empowered astral double continues to contribute empowering energy, and maintain a healing astral-physical interaction.

OBEs Interdimensional Interaction

Step 1   Apply Steps One through Four of Astral Trek to induce the desired out-of-body state.

Step 2   *Astral Memory*. While you remain in the out-of-body state, select a significant early memory from your childhood, and focus on the experience. Notice the peaceful tranquillity the memory evokes. Allow the experience, and the physical setting where it occurred, to become increasingly vivid in your mind.

Step 3   *Astral Travel*. Give yourself permission to travel to the site of the early experience. Use imagery of the target destination to guide your astral journey. Upon reaching your destination, which usually requires only a few minutes, view the physical setting from above. Note any changes in the setting which may have occurred since the early experience. Envision the early experience once again, and let yourself absorb the full pleasure of the memory.

Step 4   *Astral Light.* As the memory fades, let yourself become increasingly aware of a brilliant dimension of light in the distance. Bathed in its glow, let yourself be drawn toward the light source.

Step 5   *Power Infusion.* Upon approaching the edge of the light source, but without entering it, permit its pure energy to permeate your total being. Allow yourself to engage radiant beams of light to fill and overflow your being with power.

Step 6   *Power Transfer.* Envision your physical body at rest in the distance, and transfer overflowing power to it. Allow a stream of pure light to flow through the silver cord, to infuse your physical body with powerful energy. Fill your body to capacity with wellness and vitality. Bathe every part of your body in healing energy. Target particular areas of dysfunction or weakness, and empower them with healthy vigor.

Step 7   *Astral Return.* Without terminating the infusion process, give yourself permission to return to your physical body resting peacefully in the distance. Focusing your attention on your body and on its surroundings is usually sufficient to initiate the astral return.

Step 8   *Astral Re-entry.* End the astral experience and re-enter your physical body by focusing on breathing and other physical sensations. Before opening your eyes, affirm:

I am fully empowered.

In Step Four of this procedure, which introduces a higher dimension of light, many men and women experience a gentle, magnanimous presence, often in the form of a spiritual guide or angel. In repeated trials using this procedure, the presence typically remains unchanged. This procedure, although not designed specifically for that purpose, can be applied to identify and come to know one's spiritual guides or guardian angels.

Many persons who practice OBEs Interdimensional Interaction experience not only angels, but also the comforting presence of family members or friends who have completed their transition to the other side, particularly when the early memory involved an interaction with them. A teacher reported seeing his departed father at a distance, waving happily to him, and a psychologist reported seeing her departed child, happily playing among other children. Such interdimensional interactions are invariably empowering. They can be a source of comfort and reassurance of abundant life after death. They can also help to resolve grief resulting from the death of a loved one, particularly when the loss was sudden and unexpected.

Persons who practice this procedure often report remarkable improvements in their personal health. In the power-transfer stage, an abundance of energy is targeted in ways which energize the whole body, and increase its health resources to meet specific health needs. The results have often exceeded our most optimistic projections. A stroke patient experienced remarkable improvements in memory and command of general information, following a single application of this procedure. With repeated sessions, significant improvements were also seen in various motor skills affected by the stroke. A quadriplegic who practiced the procedure found that he experienced no discomfort or limitations during the out-of-body state. The procedure had a two-fold empowering effect: he immediately experienced a sense of internal control over his life, and within a few days, he began regaining many of his lost physical functions.

Comprehensive wellness, pain management, treatment, and rehabilitation programs of the future will hopefully include advanced concepts such as astral intervention. The quality of our lives can be profoundly enriched through health and fitness strategies which recognize the powers of our inner and outer universe, and the capacity of OBEs to engage them.

❊ 5 ❊

EMPOWERMENT
THROUGH SLEEP

Sleep is important to our mental and physical well-being for several reasons:

1. It satisfies one of our most basic physical needs.

2. It provides a gateway to the subconscious.

3. It reveals subconscious contents through dreams.

4. It offers a vehicle for spontaneous OBEs.

5. It promotes spontaneous interactions with higher planes of power.

6. It generates a physical and mental state conducive to a wide range of personal empowerment goals.

THE NATURE OF SLEEP

Although the amount of sleep the human body requires is not known, most adults tend to sleep about six to eight hours daily. The patterns of sleep, however, differ widely from person to person. Some persons require regular periods of uninterrupted sleep; others prefer brief periods which vary from day to day. Whatever the nature of our sleep patterns, when we are deprived of adequate sleep and rest for extended periods, most of us tend to lose our ability to think clearly and function effectively. We become chronically fatigued, distressed, and more susceptible to illness. Consequently, sleep assumes a critical role in our psychic-empowerment model of health and fitness.

Sleep is characterized by REM (Rapid Eye Movement) and NREM (Non-Rapid Eye Movement) cycles. Four distinct stages of NREM sleep have been identified. Stage One NREM is a very brief, transitional stage from wakefulness to sleep. It occupies only about five percent of the time we spend sleeping. Stage Two NREM occupies about half of the time for most of us, and is characterized by certain identifiable changes in electroencephalogram (EEG) waveforms. Stages Three and Four NREM, sometimes called slow-wave sleep, are the deepest levels of sleep. These stages occupy ten to twenty percent of the total time we spend asleep.

REM sleep occurs in cycles, alternating with NREM sleep at approximately ninety-minute intervals. REM sleep, during which dreaming typically occurs, occupies twenty to twenty-five percent of the total sleep time. Toward the end of the sleep period, REM sleep increases in duration. As we age, changes in sleep continuity and depth occur, such as increased wakefulness in Stage One, and a decrease in the duration of Stages Three and Four sleep.

Stage One transitional sleep offers a unique opportunity for self-empowerment intervention. Deliberately presenting suggestions during that brief, hypnotic-like stage can initiate a subconscious interaction with significant empowerment possibilities. Even in the absence of suggestions, contemplating a problem just prior to falling asleep can influence dreams to produce a quality solution. Many significant inventions and advances in science are considered products of the dream experience.

HEALTH AND FITNESS STRATEGIES

The health and fitness goals of sleep strategies are twofold: first, to promote restful sleep, and second, to intervene into the sleep experience in ways which promote wellness and stimulate dormant health potentials.

Typically, empowering sleep strategies are implemented just prior to falling asleep. Strategies focusing on restful sleep alone can also be effective in spontaneously activating dormant subconscious resources for health and fitness needs. A state of restful sleep, for instance, will often activate dream mechanisms to generate healthy energies, and disperse them throughout the body. Peaceful sleep is highly conducive to healthy OBEs and positive interactions with the higher planes of power. The restful sleep state provides optimal conditions for activating inner health potentials with health and fitness procedures.

A highly effective procedure for promoting empowering sleep is "Numbers," a strategy particularly useful for those who experience difficulty falling asleep. The procedure is based on numerology, which holds that each number has its own vibratory energy and significance beyond its simple expression of quantity. The number one represents purpose and action, while number two signifies antithesis and balance. Three stands for versatility and talent; four symbolizes solidity and steadiness; five represents adventure; six stands for dependability;

seven symbolizes mystery and knowledge; eight represents success; and nine symbolizes universal achievement.

The Numbers Procedure involves counting backwards from nine to one, as each number is visualized in some impressive way. You may, for instance, see the numbers being formed by white clouds against a peaceful blue sky, or you may imagine them being exquisitely painted by an artist on canvas. You may prefer to project the numbers boldly on the full moon, or to envision them being formed by stars in the night sky.

Each number, once it is clearly visualized, is accompanied by appropriate empowering affirmations. The affirmations, which are consistent with the number's numerological significance, can be revised, if preferred, to meet specific personal needs. In this procedure, the combination of number images and related affirmations are doubly empowering. Simply visualizing a given number within the context of its positive numerological significance can activate the number's frequency, and lead to an infusion of powerful energy. By adding appropriate affirmations to the imagery process, we can dramatically expand the procedure's empowering effects.

Numbers Procedure

Begin by lying down and, just before going to sleep, focus on your breathing. Clear your mind of active thought, then, with your eyes closed, affirm:

I am now prepared to enter peaceful, restful sleep. As I sleep, I will be protected and secure. Upon awakening, I will feel revitalized and refreshed. The powers of the numbers I envision and the affirmations I present to myself will be absorbed deeply into my subconscious mind to empower me in mind, body, and spirit.

Following this general affirmation, form a clear image of each number, one at a time. As vivid imagery of a particular number unfolds, present the affirmations relevant to that number as follows:

Number 9.

> *This number signals my oneness with the universe. All the powers of the universe are at my command. I can tap into them at any moment to energize my life with health, happiness, and fulfillment. I am now attuned to the unlimited powers of the universe. Whenever I envision the number nine, I will be instantly empowered with the positive energies of the universe.*

Number 8.

> *This number vibrates with success and fulfillment. Mentally, physically, and spiritually, I am attuned to these vibrations. I am filled with potential, and surrounded by success. The energies of this number are an integral part of my being. When I envision the number eight, I am reminded that success is my destiny.*

Number 7.

> *The number seven is the promise of continued growth and knowledge. Knowledge is power. By probing the inexhaustible mysteries of the universe, I am empowered with increased awareness and new understanding of my own life. The light of unlimited insight and enriched existence surrounds this number. By envisioning the number*

seven, I am filled with the positive energies of wholeness—a sound mind, healthy body, and soaring spirit.

Number 6.

The constancy of my identity and the totality of my being are represented by this number. I am, at this moment in time, a product of my past as well as a work in progress. From the beginning, my life has been a continuous progression of growth and an accumulation of experience. Each moment, my endless journey continues, as the unlimited opportunities of the future constantly unfold.

Number 5.

The adventures of life and the excitement of daily living are represented by the number five. Each moment of my life is filled with gladness, opportunity, and thrilling possibility. Each passing day, I discover something new about myself and the totality of my existence. I relish my existence in the here and now.

Number 4.

The vibrations of this number are firm and unwavering. They reveal the power of my inner faith and steadfast trust in myself. This number represents the constancy of my present existence and my hope for the future. I am empowered to move in unison with the universe to achieve my highest destiny. The ominous forces which threaten my existence are vulnerable to the powers of faith and trust which infuse my life with vitality, purpose, and well-being.

Number 3.

> *This number is a reminder of my unique talents and powers of adaptation. I value the richness of my life. My inner resources equip me to improve the quality of my own life, while contributing to the needs around me. I value change and new opportunities for growth and self-discovery. Even when constricted by circumstances, I will discover new options and opportunities. I am empowered to cope with adversity, and benefit from it. My powers of adaptation extend to my physical body to promote wellness and healthy biological functions. When I envision the number three, I will be instantly infused with vigor and positive energy.*

Number 2.

> *Antithesis and balance emanate from this number. Mentally and physically, I am balanced, energized, and empowered. My mind and body are exquisitely attuned to the energies of the universe. My mind is in harmony with my total being. The systems of my body are at equilibrium. I am enveloped with the glow of health and wellness. By envisioning the number two, I will immediately infuse my life with balance, health, and wellness.*

Number 1.

> *This number signifies purpose and action. My life is filled with meaning and bountiful energy. I am empowered to act and achieve. Nothing can stop me once I make up my mind. I will use my potentials to enrich my life and the lives of others.*

Whenever I envision the number one, I will be instantly empowered with purpose and vitality.

At this point, having completed the backward counting and related affirmations, you will probably be very drowsy and deeply relaxed. In fact, many persons find it difficult to remain awake long enough to complete the procedure. If you find yourself falling asleep before you finish the procedure, you can simply scan the remaining numbers as you affirm:

The powers of these numbers are now being absorbed deeply into my being.

Conclude the procedure with the following affirmation:

As I now drift into restful sleep, the power of these numbers will permeate my total being. I will remain empowered mentally, physically, and spiritually. I will awaken refreshed and revitalized.

If you remain awake following this procedure, you can facilitate sleep by imagining that you are suspended in space, perhaps on a soft, fluffy cloud drifting gently in the breeze.

PROBING THE SUBCONSCIOUS

The subconscious part of our being is a storehouse of wisdom and power. Its inexhaustible resources are accessible to our conscious probes, and its empowering processes are responsive to our active intervention. The subconscious welcomes even our most unassuming probes and willingly yields its abundant powers; however, even in the absence of any deliberate intervention effort to explore that vast region of the self, our subconscious faculties often act voluntarily and enthusiastically to enrich and empower our lives. Many of our flashes of insight come directly from the subconscious, and intuitive awareness is almost always the product of information-processing by the subconscious. The empowering skills and storage capacities of the subconscious are advanced beyond those of consciousness. They are continually engaged in efforts to generate insight, and to convey it to conscious awareness. Our greatest teacher, therapist, and psychic exist within the subconscious self.

The subconscious is attuned to cosmic forces often unknown to the conscious mind. It spontaneously engages the higher, spiritual planes of reality, and effectively transports empowering awareness of those planes to the conscious self. Our impressions of a guardian presence or the closeness of a departed loved one is often mediated by subconscious attunement to the other side. Of course, such an attunement is possible at a fully conscious level as well, but our preoccupation with the temporal and our inattentiveness to higher planes, coupled with the constrictions of sensory experience, often inhibit this transcendence to cosmic awareness. A major goal of many psychic-empowerment strategies is to raise our awareness of other dimensions, and empower us to interact with them.

In addition to its critical roles as a storage place for experience, generator of insight, and potential link to the universe, the subconscious houses many of our psychic faculties. Precognitive impressions, for instance, are often the products of subconscious dream mechanisms. Clairvoyant dreams providing specific information concerning distant realities are a clear manifestation of a subconscious psychic faculty at work. OBEs are often initiated during sleep, suggesting a subconscious faculty, or at least facilitator, for astral travel.

An important function of the subconscious is its capacity to motivate us to act. Many of our altruistic goals and commitments originate in the subconscious. For example, our strivings to relieve human or animal suffering can be seen as a product of our own past sufferings, possibly in another lifetime, but known only to the subconscious. One of our most advanced faculties is the power of the subconscious to generate positive energy, even from negative elements. If neglected, however, even our highest subconscious faculties will operate at a low level. Psychic-empowerment strategies can energize the subconscious, and generate a dynamic upward spiral of abundance and fulfillment.

Several sleep-intervention strategies have been formulated to promote health and fitness. These strategies are typically designed either to delay or arrest the earliest stage of sleep, during which empowering procedures related to health and fitness are implemented. Sleep-intervention procedures are based on a twofold premise: first, the capacity of sleep to open a gateway to the subconscious and access its vast reserve of positive power; second, the capacity of dreams to tap into specific subconscious faculties and activate them to meet particular health or physical fitness needs.

The "Gateway Intervention Procedure" accesses the positive health potentials existing in the subconscious. The procedure creates a receptive mental and physical state, while literally activating the subconscious to generate health and fitness energy. Inactive subconscious faculties are awakened, and a continuous, upward spiral of health and wellness is activated.

Gateway Intervention Procedure

Step 1 Before falling asleep, bring together the thumb and index finger tips of either hand, and hold the contact position. As you become increasingly reposed and relaxed, clear your mind by focusing on your breathing, then quietly affirm:

> *I am now calm and relaxed. As I prepare to enter*
> *peaceful sleep, I am protected and secure. I am*
> *surrounded by the glow of positive energy.*

Step 2 Disengage your fingers and imagine yourself standing at the top of a beautiful stairway, with its ten steps covered with plush carpeting. Feel the softness of the carpet under your feet. Notice, at the bottom of the stairway, a spherical light-form, glowing with positive energy, and softly bathing the stairway with light.

Step 3 As you descend the flight of stairs, counting the steps backwards one by one, let yourself become increasingly enveloped in the warm glow of energy emanating from the spherical light-form. You can sense the powerful energies permeating your body as you continue your slow descent. Take all the time you need, counting each step and sensing the plush carpet under your feet.

Step 4 Your descent now complete, step into the spherical light-form, and fully absorb its healing energies. Fill your body with the powerful warmth of wellness. Absorb the thrilling energies of health and fitness into every organ. Bathe every fiber and tendon in positive energy. Sense energy throughout your total being. You are now at your peak, physically and mentally.

Step 5 Enveloped in the wondrous sphere of energy, you are comfortable and secure. You are now ready to drift into restful, peaceful sleep. As you sleep, the infusion of energy will continue.

Step 6 Upon awakening, once again envision yourself enveloped in the glowing sphere of energy at the base of the luxurious stairway. Now, stepping from the sphere, you are ready to ascend the stairway. With each step, the infusion of power grows, spilling over to energize your total body with health and wellness.

Step 7 Your ascent now complete, rejoin your thumb and index finger as you affirm:

> *I am fully empowered mentally and physically. Throughout this day, abundant energy will be at my command. By simply engaging my thumb and index finger, I can activate bountiful energies of health and wellness.*

Step 8 Activate your inner wealth of empowering resources throughout the day by joining the tips of your thumb and index finger as you affirm:

> *I am empowered.*

You can further empower yourself by envisioning the spherical light form and yourself enveloped within it.

For best empowering results, the Gateway Intervention Procedure is practiced consecutively for several days, and then periodically. The procedure is flexible, and its contents can be varied; however, imagery of the stairway representing growth and progress, and the spherical light form representing the concentrated health and wellness powers of the subconscious, are the critical components of this procedure. They are the essential vehicles for the infusion of positive physical and mental energy.

The purpose of dream intervention is to tap into the dream experience, and use it to achieve personal-empowerment goals. Dream mechanisms are important to self-empowerment for several reasons. They initiate potentially empowering interactions between inner conscious and subconscious planes; they probe distant, outer planes of reality; they generate insight and transport it to conscious awareness; they offer quality solutions to problem situations; they challenge the dreamer to explore the innermost part of the self; and they are powerful energy generators.

Each of these dream functions is relevant to health and fitness. A positive interaction with the subconscious facilitates both mental and physical health. Interactions with higher planes access healthy energy sources; insight and quality solutions are essential to mental and physical well-being; inner awareness invariably facilitates better health; and healthy energy is a major product of the dream's creative power. Through dream intervention, we can optimize our inner resources, and promote a more fully empowered state of health and physical fitness.

The "Dream Intervention Strategy" is implemented just prior to sleep, for the purpose of either initiating empowering dream experiences, or intervening in spontaneous dreams to direct their outcomes. Both of these applications focus on dormant health resources, and build powerful images to engage our innermost powers.

Dream Intervention uses two sets of techniques. The first set is applied before falling asleep, and can be used independent of the second set, which is implemented during the dream experience itself. The first set focuses on restful sleep and dreams in an effort to promote a general state of health and well-being. The second set targets specific health needs, and generates subconscious energies to meet those needs.

DREAM INTERVENTION STRATEGY

Step 1 Upon becoming drowsy, delay sleep by spreading the fingers of one of your hands, and holding the tense, spread position.

Step 2   While holding the finger-spread position, present the following affirmation:

> *As I prepare to drift into restful sleep, I am at peace with myself and the world. I am overflowing with potential. All my inner resources are now available to me. Upon falling asleep, I will be balanced and attuned to my inner being and with the universe. All my inner resources, and all the powers of the cosmos will be available to me as I sleep. I will be infused with the energies of mental and physical well-being. My physical body will be infused with vitality and rejuvenation. My mental faculties will be energized and empowered. As I sleep, my dreams will be a source of insight and power. I will use my dreams as vehicles for health and growth.*

Step 3   Slowly release the tension in your fingers and allow the relaxation in your hand to spread into your arm and throughout your body. Affirm:

> *I now give myself permission to drift into restful, peaceful, empowering sleep.*

Step 4   As drowsiness deepens, envision your subconscious as a magical, circular pool of glowing energy, with five steps leading into it. Allow your voluntary imagery to merge with spontaneous dream images of yourself stepping into the beautiful pool of warm energy, counting the steps one by one. As you step deeper and deeper into the pool, allow the energy enveloping you to take on a radiant color. Bathe yourself in it, as you sense a oneness with the magical pool. Slowly spread the radiant energy over yourself, soaking it into your physical body. Note the wondrous energizing effects. Take plenty of time to energize the physical structures, organs, and systems of your body. Allow the glowing energy to become fully absorbed throughout your total body. Remind yourself that all things are possible to you. You can accelerate physical and mental healing; repair damaged tissue; counter the negative effects of stress on your mind and body; empower the circuitry of the central nervous system; and infuse your life with empowering thoughts, actions, and feelings.

Step 5   As sleep ensues, remind yourself that your dreams will be a source of power and insight. During dreaming, flow with the dream experience, as a channel for health and wellness.

Step 6   Upon awakening from sleep, whether suddenly to an alarm or slowly and spontaneously, once again envision the magical pool of energy and yourself at one with it. Envision, as before, the radiant energy spreading over and throughout your body, energizing every part of your being. Invigorated and fully energized, ascend from the pool, again counting the steps from one to five. Upon the count of five, affirm:

> *A pool of unlimited energy is within my being. I can draw from it at any moment to energize and empower my life with radiant health and unlimited success. I am fully energized and empowered.*

SLEEP AND HIGHER PLANES OF POWER

On this plane of temporal reality, we often experience a cosmic transcendence, in which we glimpse the higher planes of another dimension. A familiar example is the peak experience, involving the momentary lifting of awareness to a new level of profound insight. Many out-of-body experiences and meditative states open the gates to higher dimensions and experiences of new realities charged with unlimited potential for physical and mental empowerment. Experiences of *dejà vú* are often accompanied by a deep sense of wholeness or oneness with the universe. Likewise, many of our lucid dream experiences seem to engage the highest dimensions of insight and understanding. These experiences not only transcend our awareness of other realities, they inspire us with greater faith and hope for the future. The physical and mental energizing effects of these empowering experiences are often enduring.

Deep sleep provides an altered mental and physical state particularly conducive to cosmic transcendence and physical renewal. In NREM sleep Stages Three and Four, the deepest levels of sleep, our psychic being is biologically liberated to experience the highest realities, unimpeded by physical processes which are deep at rest. During these stages of non-rapid eye movement, the energies of consciousness and subconsciousness merge, thus eliminating the need for dreams as subconscious messengers. Within this state of inner oneness and in the absence of dream distractions, the potential for psychic interaction with higher dimensions is at its peak. Using appropriate strategies, the result can be a peak empowerment experience for the mind, spirit, and body.

The "Cosmic Transcendence Strategy" uses imagery and affirmation prior to sleep, to activate cosmic transcendence during the deepest stages of sleep.

COSMIC TRANSCENDENCE STRATEGY

Step 1 Before falling asleep, remind yourself of your intent to interact with higher planes. Establish a strong expectation of success. Cosmic transcendence, along with its empowering benefits, seems to happen to persons who expect it. (Good health in general is self-fulfilling—it seems to come to people who expect it. Pessimism, skepticism, and fatalism are also self-fulfilling, and invariably linked to poor health.) A success-expectancy state is formed using the following affirmations:

> *I am surrounded by opportunities and empowered with success. As I sleep, I will be infused with peaceful tranquillity and complete peace. As I enter the deepest stages of sleep, I will be composed, balanced, and in harmony within and without. All the power of the universe will be available to me. I will interact with higher planes, and draw from them all the power I need to keep me healthy and bolster my body's defense system. I welcome engagement, and invite interaction with the highest planes of power.*

At this point, these suggested affirmations can be supplemented by more specific affirmations related to a particular health issue or other concern.

Step 2 Envision the four stages of NREM sleep as planes, in varying shades of color, with each progressively intensifying in brilliance. The first stage is seen as light blue, the second stage as pale green, the third stage as soft yellow, and the fourth stage as pure white.

Step 3 Envision yourself as an energy entity with power to merge with each energy plane. Envision the first plane as a glowing, light-blue dimension of power, then affirm:

> *I am now prepared to enter deep, restful sleep. As I sleep, I will engage each colorful plane before me with confidence. I will become infused with power, as I progressively scale the planes. Upon reaching the highest plane, I will engage the highest power and wisdom of the universe. My mind, body, and spirit will be infused with the energies of good health and well-being.*

Step 4 As you continue to envision the first plane, affirm:

> *I now give myself permission to enter peaceful, restful sleep.*

Upon awakening, envision yourself enveloped in the pure white energy of the fourth plane. Affirm:

> *I am fully empowered with positive, healthy energy.*

AWAKENING EMPOWERMENT

Normal sleep is characterized by two transitional phases: falling asleep and awakening from sleep. The falling-asleep phase, called "hypnagogic sleep," is critical to sleep empowerment procedures, because it permits conscious intervention into the sleep and dreaming processes. The awakening phase of sleep, called "hypnopompic sleep," can be equally important, because it permits conscious intervention which can affect the nature of wakefulness.

Similar to post-hypnotic suggestions, interventions into either of the transitional stages of sleep can profoundly influence the normal, wakeful state. Both the Gateway Intervention Procedure and the Dream Intervention Strategy use the awakening process to reinforce the empowering effects of sleep and dream intervention procedures. Even in the absence of sleep or dream intervention, the awakening phase of sleep provides an excellent condition for empowerment procedures to dramatically influence daily life. Even when awakening is abrupt, as to an alarm, the mind and body remain transiently responsive to our conscious empowerment efforts.

The "Awakening Empowerment Strategy" capitalizes on this process by temporarily arresting it, and intervening with empowering imagery and affirmations. The procedure typically takes no more than a few minutes

AWAKENING EMPOWERMENT STRATEGY

Step 1 *Momentary Passivity.* This step is a passive mental state which allows resolution of the night's sleep experiences, including any interrupted stages or dream experiences. To facilitate transition, momentarily avoid all active thought.

Step 2 *Mind Scan.* The state of the mind is scanned as positive affirmations are formed. Positive mental elements are recognized and reinforced; all negative elements are identified and extinguished. Pessimism is replaced by optimism. Remind yourself that good things come to those who expect them. Resignation is replaced by assertion. Remind yourself that an unsinkable spirit is healthy and motivating. Hostility is replaced by good will. Remind yourself that being filled with love and good will is healthy and rewarding both mentally and physically. Conclude the mental scan with the affirmation:

I am attuned within myself and with the world.

Step 3   *Body Scan.* Scan your physical body and mentally bathe it with positive energy. This process is facilitated by imagery of a healthy glow or radiance enveloping and invigorating the body. Appropriate affirmations are then formed:

I am at my physical best. I am infused with healthy energy and vigor.

Step 4   *Activities Scan.* Mentally scan your scheduled activities for the day. Such a scan can highlight important activities and suggest possible changes in plans. Crucial precognitive and clairvoyant impressions often emerge during this scan. It is important to be spontaneous, and give attention to the mind's intuitive process. Conclude this scan with the affirmation:

I am destined for success today.

Sleep is not only a basic physical need, it is a potential gateway to the highest regions of inner and outer power. We now have numerous strategies to empower us to access those regions and maximize their empowering possibilities. To neglect sleep's empowering potentials is to neglect an exciting opportunity for enrichment in the continuous journey of growth and discovery.

❖ 6 ❖

PK POWER

Psychokinesis (PK) is the power of the mind to directly influence tangible objects, processes, conditions, and events. The PK faculty requires no external instrumentation or physical mediator. It is based on the premise that thought is energy, and once generated in sufficient form, it can be expended in ways which influence the physical world.

PK can be either spontaneous or voluntary. In its spontaneous form, PK is unsolicited, and requires no conscious effort. Voluntary PK, on the other hand, is intentional and deliberate. In its voluntary form, it is usually initiated through learned techniques designed to activate the PK faculty and direct the PK event. Unlike the voluntary form, spontaneous PK requires no mastery of PK procedures.

Whether spontaneous or voluntary, PK, like other forms of psychic phenomena, is always goal-directed and empowerment-oriented. In the controlled experimental setting, its purpose may simply be to induce motion in a pendulum object, or influence the fall of dice; however, even these laboratory exercises are empowerment oriented.

They manifest the power of the mind in a highly objective, observable mode. Moreover, they exercise and strengthen the PK faculty.

PK IN THE LABORATORY AND CLASSROOM

Laboratory investigations of PK are important for at least three reasons. First, if PK can be demonstrated under controlled laboratory conditions, instances of spontaneous PK in everyday life become more explainable. Second, investigations of PK in the laboratory yield important information concerning the controllable nature of the faculty and ways of developing it. Finally, laboratory studies of PK suggest many important applications of the phenomenon, including its usefulness in promoting physical health and personal development.

Several of our laboratory studies successfully demonstrated the power of the mind to influence tangible objects. In a controlled demonstration of group PK, six volunteer subjects drawn from a college-student population, were successful in moving a pendulum that was suspended under a bell jar on a laboratory table. Three subjects were seated on each side of the table. A metronome was placed at one end of the table to pace their alternate efforts to push against the pendulum, or pull it toward them. As one group mentally pushed the pendulum away, the other group mentally pulled it forward. A turning motion of the pendulum object was first noted, then a distinct to-and-fro movement. The metronome was then stopped to allow the moving pendulum to pace the push-and-pull efforts of the two groups. The motion of the pendulum rapidly accelerated, until it struck the sides of the bell jar. To stop the pendulum, the groups reversed their efforts by pushing against the pendulum when it moved toward them, and pulling it when it moved away from them. Almost immediately, they brought the pendulum to a complete stop.

In another controlled study, the self-ratings of successful-versus-unsuccessful PK subjects were compared. Forty-four volunteer college students were given the task of individually producing motion in a pendulum suspended under a laboratory bell jar. Of the forty-four subjects, twenty-six succeeded in producing distinct motion in the pendulum. Self-ratings of the successful-versus-unsuccessful subjects revealed:

1. The successful subjects, without exception, reported that they expected to succeed in producing motion in the pendulum. Only two of the eighteen unsuccessful subjects expected the pendulum to respond.

2. Twenty-four of the twenty-six successful subjects reported that they were "always" or "almost always" in control of their lives. Only five of the unsuccessful subjects reported such a degree of control.

3. Without exception, the successful subjects reported that they "always" set their own goals; the unsuccessful subjects reported either "usually" or "almost never" setting their own goals.

4. Without exception, the successful subjects said they were "always" or "almost always" in control of events around them; only four of the unsuccessful subjects reported such a degree of control.

5. Without exception, the successful subjects reported that they "always" made their own decisions. Only three of the unsuccessful subjects reported this.

6. Compared to the unsuccessful subjects, the successful subjects reported a higher frequency of spontaneous OBEs outside the laboratory.

7. Without exception, the successful subjects reported sensations of pleasure and a heightened state of physical prowess upon inducing motion in the pendulum.

8. All participants of the study believed that the PK ability, if developed, could be a highly practical and useful tool.

In our follow-up studies, both the successful and unsuccessful experimental subjects rapidly improved their PK skills when given instruction and guided practice. In fact, some of the unsuccessful subjects in our earlier experiments progressed so rapidly, that they surpassed their successful counterparts in later PK experiments. These findings suggest that, with practice designed to exercise our PK skills, we can all acquire a higher level of PK empowerment, and greater effectiveness in using this important faculty to achieve personal empowerment, including health and physical fitness goals.

Exercising the PK faculty does not require a sophisticated, controlled, laboratory setting. Many everyday situations provide excellent opportunities. Common examples are producing movement among the leaves of a plant or in the folds of a curtain. Objects that reflect light are particularly conducive to PK. A chandelier, with its hanging prisms, the still surface of water, and even a cloud in the sky, provide excellent practice situations. Exercises such as flipping a coin and tossing dice offer further opportunities. Practicing a variety of strategies under wide-ranging conditions will eventually produce observable PK.

In psychic development, the simplest exercise is often the most effective. In a dramatic classroom demonstration of PK power, a group of college students, enrolled in a parapsychology seminar, induced a brief turning motion, then full levitation in a crumpled mass of aluminum foil which had been placed on a table in front of them. In another classroom PK exercise, students used their PK powers to move a pencil from the center of a desk to the desk's edge, whereupon their influence pushed it to the floor.

Students experience PK Levitation in a classroom experiment.

PK outside the laboratory is not uncommon. In accident situations, it can slow the fall of a dropped object to prevent damage, or it can literally slow one's own fall. An equestrienne reported slowing her fall to avoid injury after being thrown from her horse. Similarly, a construction worker, upon falling from a scaffold, reportedly escaped injury by slowing the fall and cushioning its impact. Many persons involved in accidents or near-accidents report spontaneously entering the out-of-body state, during which they deliberately influenced the dangerous situation as it unfolded below them. A student, upon slipping as he stepped from his shower, instantly entered the out-of-body state, during which he slowed his fall, and maneuvered his body away from the dangerous edge of the tiled shower opening. Such instances of PK intervention in daily life suggest the powerful potential of this faculty to promote our physical well-being.

PK IN HEALTH AND FITNESS

The application of PK to health and fitness is based on the premise that a psychic faculty capable of influencing external events could, logically, and perhaps with even greater ease, influence internal biological events. Such a concept suggests an extensive range of empowering possibilities for promoting our physical well-being. Repairing damaged tissue, regulating dysfunctional systems, building resistance to illness, and helping organs to be healthier and function better are only a few examples of the potential health benefits. A major challenge facing us today is the mastery of PK skills and the deliberate use of them to unlock our potentials for good health, and enrich the quality of our lives.

The mind is master of the body. Positive thoughts and empowered mental states invariably promote good health. We can literally think ourselves healthy. The biological effects of positive thoughts and mental states illustrate the forcefulness of the mind and its power to influence matter—in this case, the physical body and its functions. This phenomenon is an example of PK power at its peak.

Unfortunately, the powers of the mind, if left unattended, or even worse, if misdirected, can have disempowering effects on the physical body. Examples of this are chronic stress that, given time, damages body tissue and wears out organs; a defeatist, pessimistic attitude weakening the body's defense and immune systems; smoldering hostility resulting in greater susceptibility to a variety of illnesses, including the nation's number one killer—heart disease. It would follow that, taking control of these negative states and reversing them would likewise reverse their disempowering effects and promote good health. An internal locus of control or a prevailing attitude of being in charge of your life, is inherently empowering. It is, in fact, the essential foundation of empowering PK.

Like many of our other psychic faculties, PK is never at complete rest; it is always on line and ready to respond to our interaction. Our natural predisposition, however, is toward minimal use, if not utter neglect, of this empowering faculty. Only when PK is dramatically activated, such as in an emergency situation, do many of us become aware of this remarkable inner power.

ACTIVATING HEALTHFUL PK

The PK faculty responds to intervention efforts which focus on the prerequisites for empowering PK. Certain underlying conditions are known to provide a strong foundation for psychic growth and the development of specific psychic potentials. For instance, feelings of personal worth, high self-esteem, an orientation toward success, and, as already noted, a strong internal locus of control, are conditions which invariably promote our psychic unfoldment. They also promote good physical and mental health. In our psychic empowerment model of health and fitness, cultivating these underlying conditions is an essential step toward developing our potentials and becoming a fully empowered person.

The "PK Prescription for Health and Fitness" identifies empowering personality traits and specific elements which facilitate positive, spontaneous PK intervention into biological systems. A major objective of the procedure is to advance harmony within the self, while promoting heightened awareness and attunement to the self's empowering essence. Attention is focused on the mental states and processes required to spontaneously activate healthy PK mechanisms, and release the flow of positive energy to foster health. Through introspection, disabling thoughts are identified and replaced with positive, rational thoughts. The mental and physical expressions of failure are intercepted and corrected. Disempowering attitudes and emotions are disarmed and reversed.

The four-step procedure is essentially cognitive in nature, requiring a comfortable setting, free of distractions, for a period of approximately thirty minutes.

THE PK PRESCRIPTION PROCEDURE

Step 1 *Affirmation*. As you settle back and relax, affirm your goal of becoming more fully empowered, with the capacity to use your PK potentials for good health:

> *My goal is to become an empowered person. I am prepared to take command of my life and bring forth positive change. I am becoming balanced with my true self. I am discovering the essence of my inner being. My PK faculties are now available to me. I will find ways to tap into my psychic powers and release them to enrich my life with health and wellness.*

> *I am capable of changing my life. By looking inward, I will discover my true inner self and its positive potentials. I will replace the toxic waste of negative attitudes and emotions with positive, empowering resources. I will reverse negative thoughts with positive affirmations. I will unleash new growth potential in my life.*

Step 2 *Focusing*. The objective of this step is to focus introspectively on existing attitudes, beliefs, and emotions, in an effort to identify, examine, and replace disempowering elements with empowering ones. Areas of focus include, but are not limited to, the following:

- *The Inner Self.* Identify specific disempowering concepts and expectations. Remind yourself that you are an individual of dignity and incomparable worth. Remind yourself that you have an unlimited supply of inner resources. Tell yourself emphatically, *I love who I am.* Uproot expectations of failure and toss them out.

- *Beliefs.* Identify disempowering beliefs. Banish and replace them with positive convictions. Remind yourself that you do not have to be all things to all people. Being true to yourself is more important than pleasing others. View your imperfections as challenges, not irreversible faults. Think of your problems as opportunities, not barriers. Think of your failures and misfortunes as temporary set-backs, not horrible disasters. Remind yourself that success, like life, is a process, not a product. Tell yourself that you are a work in progress. Remind yourself that, as you grow and develop, you are succeeding. Recognize your weaknesses, but do not use them as excuses; use your strengths to compensate for your weaknesses. Remind yourself that you are a self-made person. The world, the culture, and your environment provide the raw material, but you build your own life. You are what you choose to be.

- *Emotions.* Remind yourself that your feelings are important and worth listening to. Get them out and address them. Become aware of them as valid expressions of your innermost self. Pay attention to your negative, as well as positive feelings. Use positive self-talk to build feelings of worth and expectations of success. Expressing yourself is healthy and empowering, both mentally and physically.

• *Attitude.* The empowerment attitude asserts, *I am filled with unlimited potential and surrounded by unlimited opportunities.* The empowerment attitude is a "take-charge" state of mind. It is solution-oriented rather than problem-centered. It emphasizes positive possibilities, rather than negative probabilities. It looks at the total situation, not the down side only. It copes actively with adversity, rather than passively yielding to it. It views even personal suffering as potentially empowering. It finds opportunities for choice and room for action even in the most restrictive situation. The empowerment attitude can be summed up with the positive affirmation, *I am empowered.* With frequent use, that affirmation becomes more and more empowering.

On the surface, focusing on the self, beliefs, emotions, and attitudes may seem unrelated to PK. Remember, however, that by generating the positive conditions conducive to PK, you unlock inner sources of health and prepare the PK faculty to distribute powerful healing and wellness energy throughout your body.

Step 3   *Infusion.* The focusing step now complete, assume a
         reflective state of mind, and allow the empowerment
         products of focusing to be absorbed into the innermost
         part of your self. Envision the central core of your
         being as a powerful, glowing magnet, attracting posi-
         tive energy, while repelling anything negative. Allow a
         few moments for this infusion process to complete
         itself. As the reflective state continues, allow your PK
         powers to become activated to disperse health and
         vitality throughout your body. Allow physical organs
         and functions to be spontaneously targeted and
         infused with healthy energy.

Another highly effective strategy for activating PK and focusing it
on health and fitness targets, is the four-step "PK Formula for Health
and Fitness."

PK FORMULA FOR HEALTH AND FITNESS

Step 1   *Sensate Focusing.* Center your full attention on your
         physical body and its sensations. With your eyes
         closed, notice areas of coolness, warmth, tension, tin-
         gling, numbness, and pressure. Zero in on specific sen-
         sations, study them, and practice altering them. For
         example, replace coolness with warmth, tension with
         relaxation. Substitute numbness for tingling, and move
         pressure points to other locations. Allow the various
         sensations to become smooth and pleasurable.

Step 2   *Energizing PK Systems.* As your eyes remain closed,
         energize your physical and mental systems by mentally
         scanning your body from your head downward as you
         envision a soft blanket of glowing energy accompanying

the scan and enveloping your body. Breathe deeply as you envision a powerful core of pulsating energy in your solar plexus region. Allow the energy generated by the central core to permeate your total body with its vibrance and radiance.

Step 3   *Balancing PK Systems.* To balance your PK energy systems, bring the tips of your fingers together in a praying-hands position. Hold the position for a few moments as you affirm:

> *I am energized and balanced with PK power.*

Sense the balancing exchange of powerful energy at your fingertips. You are now at your energized peak.

Step 4   *PK Energy Release.* Center your full attention on the PK target—internal organs, biological systems, or fitness goals. As you focus on the target, envision the desired PK outcomes. Allow a powerful beam of PK energy to permeate the target. Permit the energy release to intensify in brilliance, as needed, to achieve the desired results. Close down the energy release by again focusing on the central energy core of your solar plexus region. Affirm:

> *I am empowered with the energies of health and fitness.*

The PK Formula for Health and Fitness, requires approximately thirty minutes, and can be adapted to any health and fitness need. While not essential, relevant knowledge of physiology facilitates application of this procedure.

Although the PK Formula was developed specifically for health and fitness needs, it is a highly effective procedure for exercising the

Balancing PK Systems

PK faculty using outward targets. For this application, an external situation is the focal point for energy release, rather than the physical body.

In its broadest, yet somewhat controversial application, PK can be used in ways which affect other persons, and, when applied on a massive scale, conceivably to influence group behavior and even global conditions. Such a potentially powerful application of PK demands certain ethical considerations and a careful examination of purpose. The psychic empowerment model of health and fitness emphasizes the incomparable worth of all human beings and the importance of responsible choice. Promoting our own well-being, and that of others, is the cardinal principle underlying all psychic empowerment. That principle must guide our psychic development and any application of our psychic faculties on a broader scale.

Harmony with the true inner self and attunement to its essence are the critical conditions for generating a positive energy force to influence conditions within ourselves and around us. Given an empowered psychic system, we can effectively disperse empowering energy as well as receive it. By sending empowering energy to benefit others, we exercise our psychic faculties and build our inner empowerment resources. We become more effective in sending and receiving empowering energy, while repelling any disempowering influence.

Positive thought energy, once generated, has a cumulative, empowering effect. It elicits positive responses, repels negative forces, and produces positive consequences. Positive energy dispersed inwardly empowers the self. When directed outwardly, it empowers others. When dispersed into the universe, it empowers the planet. It can even be dispersed into infinity, where its cumulative effects know no limits. When expended to meet empowerment goals, positive energy eventually returns to us several-fold.

Unfortunately, negative thought energy tends also to be cumulative. When dispersed inwardly against the self, it disempowers the mind and body. When sent outwardly against others, it returns in multiplied form to disempower the sender. When dispersed globally, it can gather as a toxic cloud of darkness over the planet. Global conflict, injustice, hunger, and war can be seen as the cumulative effects of negative energy generated on a massive scale.

Fortunately, positive thought energy will invariably overpower its negative counterpart. Massive negative accumulations, however, cry out for massive countermeasures. An unhealthy, polluted planet, whose resources are recklessly exploited, demands our attentive and responsive intervention on a global scale. Disempowered populations, devastated by discrimination, exploitation, and poverty, implore action of the empowered populations of the world.

The accumulation of negative energy from the past requires positive intervention to release its destructive forcefulness. We can each contribute to that collective effort by first, maximizing our inner psychic capacity and promoting our own personal growth, and second, actively dispersing positive energy and applying our psychic resources to make the world a better place.

The collective consciousness of nations and groups can shape world events. The survival of oppressed nations throughout history is often attributed to the unsinkable spirit of people who simply refused to give up. Their means of survival were, at times, purely psychic. During World War II, gifted psychics across England gathered regularly, and used their PK powers to deflect German V-2 rockets from the country's heavily populated areas. Similarly, England's crippling defeat of the Great Spanish Armada in 1588 has been partly attributed to groups of psychics who, gathering at the sea, used their PK powers to embolden the English fleet, and later, to spawn storms which battered the Armada, thus effectively ending Spain's command of the seas.

Religious traditions abound with detailed accounts of extraordinary events suggesting PK: bodies of water separated, rods turned into serpents, fire rendered harmless, jaws of lions locked shut, messages carved into stone, prison gates shaken ajar, fishes and loaves multiplied, storms at sea calmed, and even the rotation of the planet halted. Such events, whether the product of human interaction with a higher dimension of power, or the direct result of a purely human capacity, suggest unlimited PK possibilities. Past and present accounts of PK as spiritual or miraculous events offer a widely accepted explanation of the phenomenon, while at the same time, validating its existence and justifying its various manifestations, often in critical life and death situations.

ENERGIZING THE GLOBE

A rational extension of PK as a health and fitness strategy is the application of PK toward making the world a safer, healthier place. A polluted environment is dangerous to our health, and violence is a threat to our safety. We recklessly contaminate the air, defile our rivers and streams, and set in motion a host of destructive forces which disempower the globe. All too often, we see a wanton disregard for human rights and an absence of compassion for others. These conditions have already exacted a heavy toll on the quality of life of this planet. The survival of the world is at stake. Technologically, we have the capacity to destroy the earth in a heartbeat. Psychically, we have the power to energize and revitalize it. A major challenge facing the psychically empowered today is decisive intervention into the gathering darkness of toxicity enveloping the globe.

The "Global Intervention Procedure" is a PK strategy designed to bathe the planet in revitalizing energy and meet particular earth needs. Psychic intervention on a global scale focuses on three specific objectives:

1. Identify and block destructive global forces, thereby preventing further disempowerment of the planet.

2. Correct toxic global conditions and reverse their damaging effects.

3. Raise global awareness, promote appreciation of the planet, and prompt positive action on a global scale.

The Global Intervention Procedure can be used individually or in groups. In global empowerment, our individual efforts unite with a larger energy force, already set in motion by the empowerment contributions of other individuals and groups. The effectiveness of any empowerment effort depends, in the final analysis, on individual commitment and participation; however, the empowerment efforts of a larger group would logically create a more synergistic empowering effect.

GLOBAL INTERVENTION PROCEDURE

For this procedure, a globe is recommended to facilitate the empowerment effort. In the group setting, the globe is situated near the center of the group, and the group members are usually seated in a circular arrangement. Specific earth needs are discussed, and goals are formulated by the group. In addition to general objectives, such as global peace and ending human and animal suffering, the procedure can include a wide range of highly specific objectives, such as strengthening the weakened ozone layer, revitalizing forests damaged by acid rain, and empowering an endangered species, to list but a few of the possibilities.

Step 1 With the globe visible to all participants, the planet is personalized and addressed, in unison if preferred, with affirmations similar to the following:

As the living planet, you are a part of us, and we are a part of you. Your well-being facilitates our well-being. The healthy conditions which empower you also empower us. The toxic forces which weaken you likewise weaken us. You give support and power to us daily. We now give support and power to you. We enfold you with positive energy and the light of peace.

These affirmations of caring and commitment are usually followed by moments of silence, and images of the

Global Intervention Procedure

planet surrounded with the glow of invigorating energy. An active effort is made to infuse the earth with powerful energy. Turning the palms of the hands toward the globe facilitates the infusion effort.

Step 2 In the next stage of the procedure, attention is focused on more specific empowerment objectives. Appropriate empowering affirmations are presented, as desired effects are envisioned. For example, revitalizing a devastated forest could include envisioning the near-dead forest and addressing it with the affirmation:

You are now revitalized with powerful growth energy.

Follow this with imagery of the forest coming alive with towering trees, prolific foliage, lush undergrowth, and teeming animal life. We can further personalize our empowerment efforts by envisioning ourselves as part of the energized forest, interacting with its wondrous mix of excitement and tranquillity.

PK, on a global scale, is important because of its capacity to initiate a global rebuilding process. Equally as important are the motivational effects of our global PK efforts. By actively intervening into global problems through PK, we discover other ways to create global change, and reverse the onslaught of destructive forces which disempower the earth.

7

The Psychic Tools of Health and Fitness

The physical body is an incredible creation. It consists of countless parts effectively interacting and working together.

- The heart and circulatory system distribute oxygen to every cell of the body;

- Bones, arranged in a masterful framework, provide a solid support system.

- Muscles, tendons, joints, and supportive tissue give motion to the body.

- The brain and nervous system consist of forty billion neurons extending to every part of the body.

- Hormones form a complex control system for regulating activities.

- Connective tissue, nerves, and blood cells work together to build and rebuild the body.

- The immune, digestive, reproductive, and other highly intricate systems, are all elegantly designed to function in perfect synchronicity.

Even more astounding than the physical body is the amazing structure of our inner being. Our destiny as human beings is not determined by our physical makeup, nor by the hereditary and environmental forces which shape it. Neither is it forged somewhere in the outer universe, nor molded on some distant plane. It is determined by the choosing self. Given the powerful pen of the indestructible inner self, we can write our own life script. The incredible power of our innermost being exceeds all the wonders of the physical body and the other remarkable feats of nature seen throughout the universe. We can choose empowerment over disempowerment, success over failure, and mastery over mediocrity.

The psychic-empowerment model of health and fitness offers many important strategies designed to promote our physical and mental well-being. Just as important as these empowering procedures are the numerous psychic tools we can use to enrich our lives, and on a larger scale, to help make the world a better place. The tools of psychic empowerment are typically tangible objects with the capacity to access sources of psychic power and activate our psychic potentials when properly applied. These tools function in several ways:

1. They can stimulate our inner psychic faculties and initiate empowering psychic processes, including those related to health and fitness.

2. They can evoke rich imagery, which provides the basis for empowering mental and physical interactions.

3. They can link conscious awareness to the subconscious sources of insight and power.

4. They can provide a tangible point of focus around which we can muster our psychic powers.

5. They can probe distant sources of knowledge and power.

6. They can promote a positive state of mind and a success-expectancy effect, conditions considered essential to many psychic empowerment goals.

7. They can generate an empowered, revitalized physiological state.

8. They can function as instruments of other dimensions to channel knowledge and power to the self.

9. They can engage an empowering interaction between the physical and non-physical dimensions of our existence.

The use of tangible objects as empowering tools has a long and interesting history. Archaeological excavations have uncovered countless artifacts which depict humankind's early struggle for power. Frequently, these tangible objects were seen as either symbols or mystical sources of power. Common examples were ceremonial items such as masks, weapons, and tools, along with various sculpted objects representing supernatural forces, deities, and other distant powers.

Today, the use of tangible objects to signify power continues unabated. Among the examples are a vast range of material possessions—stocks, bonds, money, and real estate—as indices of status, power, and success; diplomas, citations, and awards symbolizing a variety of personal accomplishments; and various religious objects signifying faith or a divine presence.

Many tangible objects are empowering because of their motivational or inspirational significance. Tangibles such as trophies and medals recognize our personal accomplishments and motivate us to strive for even higher levels of achievement. They are often prominently displayed as evidence of past success and manifestations of future possibilities. At another level, a national flag, as a symbol of freedom, can inspire patriotism and even sacrifice. When accompanied by affirmations of allegiance, it becomes doubly empowering. Similarly, objects of religious significance can serve as symbols of commitment, as well as tools of inspiration.

Beyond their symbolic and associative values, many objects or tangible conditions seem to possess autonomous empowering properties. Consequently, they can be directly empowering, independent of their symbolic significance. Examples are a centuries-old cathedral which connects us to our past, and energizes us with hope for the future; a towering mountain which, by its existence alone, impels us to scale its heights; a magnificent sunset which lifts consciousness to a higher plane; or a special place in nature, where we go for inspiration and renewal. The direct empowering consequences of such interactions can be deep and profoundly enduring.

Along another line, many precious and semi-precious gems are valued for their direct, autonomous, empowering properties. When worn as ornaments, some of them are thought to emit healthy energies, or at least to stimulate a psychic interaction to promote health and revitalize the body. Amethyst, for instance, is valued for its inherent capacity to channel healing and wellness. Amber is valued by many competitive athletes for its usefulness in building physical endurance. Many body builders and weight lifters have found that black coral accelerates muscle development and improves competitive performance. Jade has been associated with improved motor coordination and technical excellence in complex skills such as ballet and figure skating. Topaz is valued for its effectiveness in building the body's immune and defense systems.

The emerald is believed to emit rejuvenating energies, and is thus associated with longevity. In our interviews with centenarians, the emerald was typically identified as their favorite gem. Interestingly, the diamond appears to possess little health and fitness value; in fact, this popular gem is believed to emit weakening energies which can disrupt aura frequencies, and actually harm health. In the sports setting, the diamond can impair motor coordination, and generate fatigue which interferes with performance. Large, flawless diamonds are believed to generate intensely negative frequencies considered to be particularly disempowering. Misadventure, illness, and tragedy often accompany the prolonged wearing of this gem.

Certain clothing fabrics, like certain gems, are thought to possess potentially empowering health and fitness properties. Natural fibers are generally considered more conducive to health and fitness than synthetics or synthetic-blends. Cotton, wool, silk, and flax, as well as blends of these materials, are believed to be among the healthiest fibers, and do not adversely alter the body's energy system.

Our studies of the human aura revealed that some human-made materials, including plastics and tightly woven synthetics, can constrict the aura, and disrupt its symmetry. Although these effects vary from individual to individual, prolonged exposure to any condition which interrupts the healthy aura will almost always assert a wear-and-tear effect on both mind and body. Among the common reactions to these conditions are chronic fatigue, muscular tension, anxiety, despondency, and sexual dysfunction.

The color of fabrics, like the fabrics themselves, can interact with the aura system to affect health and physical fitness. Typically, colors or color combinations which complement the aura will help us look and feel better. Colors which clash with the aura also clash with the physiology. The most reliable index to healthy clothing colors and fabrics is our mental and physical reactions to the garment as we wear it.

Fatigue is the first symptom of the misuse of fabrics and colors, an effect we can readily reverse by simply changing to aura-compatible clothing. Many of us may have made the mistake of selecting an expensive, but aura-incompatible garment, and possibly never wearing it, or at most, wearing it only once. Unfortunately, our reactions are not always noticeable and immediate, but often subtle and delayed, while their effects can be cumulative. As a general rule, our favorite materials and colors offer a reasonably reliable guide to selecting healthy garments.

Some aura systems are highly color-sensitive; other systems are almost completely insensitive to color. The dominantly orange aura typically has high color sensitivity, and is particularly reactive to certain shades of red and green. The dominantly blue aura, on the other hand, has little color sensitivity. The light-blue aura will accommodate clothing of any color, with no adverse effects. Not surprisingly, the most successful high-fashion models almost invariably have light blue auras. The dominantly green aura is color sensitive to orange and shades of red. The dominantly yellow aura is somewhat color sensitive to shades of red, pink, and purple.

Blue and white are the universal colors of high style, good health, and physical fitness. These fabric colors are compatible and energizing to auras of all colors and characteristics. A clothing combination of dark blue and white is not only stylish, but healthy, and typically complimentary for both men and women. Our survey of careers requiring uniforms, including the military, found that job satisfaction was greatest for careers with blue and/or white uniforms. Job satisfaction was lowest for those careers requiring brown or gray uniforms.

Purchasing personal garments by assessing their effects on the aura is both health-empowering and style-enhancing. Incompatible colors and fabrics will constrict, disrupt, or discolor the aura. Because the effects of color and fabric are clearly observable in the aura surrounding the hands, the Aura Hand Viewing Technique, discussed in Chapter Five, is a highly effective procedure for assessing these influences. Some upscale retailers now provide special aura-viewing areas, with appropriate screen and lighting, to assess the effects of particular fabrics and colors on the aura. A few highly exclusive establishments provide professional aura consultants who assist clients—men and women—to select garments which complement and energize their auras.

In our research, the color and fabric environment of sleep was found to be particularly relevant to health and fitness. Bed coverings and sleeping apparel of aura-compatible colors contribute significantly to healthy, invigorating sleep. As a rule, white and pale shades of color are conducive to restful sleep and pleasant dreaming. Our studies found that dark brown and black fabrics are almost always disruptive to sleep. Rapid improvements were noted among persons with sleep disturbances, including various dyssomnias and parasomnias, when their sleep environment was made more aura-compatible. Mood state, likewise, was influenced by the sleep environment. As expected, a positive mood state was associated with an aura-compatible environment. It is important to note that the empowering and disempowering effects of the sleep environment are cumulative in nature. Because we spend so much of our lives sleeping, a healthy sleeping environment is critical to our mental and physical well-being.

HEALTHFUL PSYCHIC TOOLS
AND STRATEGIES

The psychic tools used for promoting health and physical fitness include an array of tangibles often coupled with universally accepted empowering strategies such as positive affirmation and related mental imagery. The same psychic tools and procedures we use to stimulate clairvoyance and precognition, are also known to promote better physical and mental health. As we develop and practice our psychic skills, we indirectly revitalize the mind and body.

Reaching beyond the side-benefits of other psychic techniques, strategies using a variety of tangible tools have been developed to directly promote better health and fitness. Among the more commonly used are the familiar crystal ball, the pyramid, quartz crystals, and various personalized objects.

The Crystal Ball

The crystal ball is both an object of beauty and an instrument of potential power. Crystal gazing, or scrying, the primary strategy involving this tool, has its roots in antiquity. Although it has often been associated with fortune telling and the occult, crystal gazing has, in recent years, commanded the interest of researchers. It has gained recognition as a potentially empowering procedure with a host of valuable applications.

In laboratory studies, improved performance in telepathy, clairvoyance, and precognition was noted when crystal gazing was introduced into the experimental situation. These studies further revealed that crystal gazing actively stimulates creative thinking, increases motivation, and reduces stress. When practiced regularly, it can rapidly accelerate the rate of learning and improve retention. As a health and fitness tool, it can help balance physical systems and keep the parts of the body working in harmony.

Crystal gazing typically requires a quiet setting with the crystal ball situated on a table at a comfortable distance from the gazer to facilitate viewing at a slightly downward angle. In the group setting, the crystal ball is placed near the center of the group, with the group members seated in a circle. A clear view of the crystal ball is critical to the procedure.

Crystal Gazing

One of the most effective crystal-gazing procedures, with the widest range of potential benefits, is "Spontaneous Gazing." The procedure is initiated by relaxing the body, clearing the mind of active thought, and focusing on the crystal ball. Viewing continues for a period of approximately thirty minutes, interspersed with brief intervals of rest, during which the eyes are closed as needed. This procedure is particularly useful as a stress-management strategy.

Spontaneous Gazing is recommended prior to any potentially stressful event, such as a performance, presentation, or job interview. College students find this procedure highly effective when practiced immediately prior to course examinations. Journalism students who used Spontaneous Gazing reported a marked increase in the flow of creative ideas. In the business setting, a significant increase in job satisfaction followed the implementation of this procedure as an experimental strategy. Managers who practiced the procedure daily, reported improved interpersonal relations and greater effectiveness in achieving their management goals. Heightened mental alertness, increased self-confidence, and a strong state of success-expectancy are among the other reported benefits of Spontaneous Gazing.

Crystal gazing, as applied to health and fitness, consists of spontaneous gazing supplemented by structured procedures, including appropriate imagery and empowering affirmations. "Fitness Through Gazing" is a procedure that centers on specific health and fitness goals, and uses the crystal ball as an energizing focal point.

FITNESS THROUGH GAZING

Step 1 Following a brief period of slowed breathing and physical relaxation, allow your mind to become passive as you focus on the crystal ball.

Step 2 Continue gazing for several minutes. Notice the peacefulness and serenity enveloping you as you focus your full attention on the crystal ball. Allow yourself to become momentarily lost in the gazing experience. Permit yourself to enjoy the experience to its fullest.

Step 3 Close your eyes and review your health and fitness goals, envisioning them as clearly as possible. If your goal is to build your body's defense system, envision your body glowing with power. Picture dark invaders being fought off by warriors of light. Imagine your body as an incredible machine, with every part working smoothly and with perfect precision. To empower particular organs, envision the organ, and bathe it with powerful light. Note the revitalization process as it occurs. For a particular body system, such as the cardiovascular system, picture the fabric of your body from head to foot, every thread radiant with energy.

Step 4 With your eyes remaining closed, formulate powerful affirmations related to your health and fitness goals:

> *I am totally empowered with the energies of health. My physical organs and systems are working in perfect harmony. The nutrient centers of my body are open. My body is tuned and ready. I am at my peak of physical power.*

Step 5 Open your eyes and resume crystal gazing. Imagine the crystal ball as a powerful generator of health and wellness energy. Envision a beam of glowing energy connecting your solar plexus region to the center of the crystal ball. Mentally engage a powerful energy infusion by envisioning your body's energy system radiating with new energy. Let yourself sense the physical build-up of inner power. Permit the infusion of energy to permeate every cell, fiber, tendon, and bone of your body.

Step 6 Close your eyes and allow the infusion process to reach its highest peak. Conclude with the affirmation:

> *I am empowered.*

Fitness Through Gazing can be practiced daily, or as frequently as preferred. An evening hour just prior to sleep is ideal for this procedure. Sleep provides the optimal condition for continuing and intensifying the infusion process initiated during crystal gazing.

A second strategy, called "Mutual Crystal Gazing," can be used to generate a positive energy exchange between two participants. This

procedure has important implications for health and physical fitness, as well as for mental empowerment. Based on the concept of
entropy and equivalence, the procedure holds that two unequally
charged bodies, when in juxtaposition, give off and receive energy
until a state of equilibrium is reached. Mutual Crystal Gazing provides for the exchange of positive energy only. Any introduction of
negative energy automatically closes down the exchange process.
Since it is empowering to give as well as receive positive energy, both
participants benefit from the exchange procedure.

Mutual Crystal Gazing

A crystal ball is placed at the center of a table between
two participants who face each other.

Step 1   Following a brief period of spontaneous crystal gazing
and introspection, the two participants join hands at
each side of the crystal ball. One hand of each participant is then turned palm-side up and the other hand
turned palm-side down so that the palms of one participant rests in an interfaced, contact position with the
palms of the other participant.

Step 2   Alternately and spontaneously, each participant affirms
the objectives of the exercise as crystal gazing continues. Examples of appropriate affirmations are:

> *We are open to this empowering interaction and
> exchange of positive energy. As we give positive
> energy, we will also receive positive energy. The
> energy exchange will increase itself many-fold.
> We will be empowered mentally and physically
> by this experience.*

Mutual Crystal Gazing

Step 3 With eyes closed, both participants activate their energy systems by visualizing light flowing into the interfaced palms, which provide the functional area for a powerful energy exchange. As the exchange procedure continues, sensations of becoming dynamically energized are noted, not only in the palms, but throughout the total body.

Step 4 For specific health and fitness needs, the participants together envision the physical organ, function, or system to be energized, then mutually release positive energy to envelop and become absorbed into that region.

Step 5 The hands of both participants are then placed palm sides down on the crystal ball. An image is formed of a powerful stream of energy from overhead, entering the crystal ball, then radiating into the hands and through-out the body of each participant.

Step 6   The procedure is concluded with the affirmation:

> *We are now fully energized with positive health and fitness energy. We are fully empowered, both mentally and physically.*

A brief period of reflection and continued relaxation intensifies the empowering effects of this procedure.

The Pyramid

Heading the list of the great architectural wonders of the world is the pyramid. For centuries, it has stood as a universal symbol of power and mystery. Although the pyramid was found among various ancient cultures, the best known of these magnificent structures is the Great Pyramid erected at the direction of Pharaoh Khufu (Cheops) in the 2600s B.C.E., near Cairo, Egypt.

The Great Pyramid, with its exquisite beauty and exactness of design, remains a challenging enigma. Incredibly, the ratio of its height to the perimeter of its base equals almost exactly the ratio of the radius of a circle to its circumference. That record of geometric fact, along with certain amazing meteorological features found in its design, only deepens the mystery of this astounding architectural feat. Today, we continue to probe its secrets. Some contemporary Egyptologists speculate that, with the capstone in place, the Great Pyramid may have served as an energy generator. Many contemporary industrial and commercial buildings, as well as residential structures, have features of the pyramid integrated into their designs, and some have replicas of the Great Pyramid imbedded in their foundations to generate a positive energy field.

Apart from the mystery and the many claims of power that surround the Great Pyramid, small-scale replicas of this architectural wonder have demonstrated remarkable empowerment potential. The effectiveness of the replica as an empowering tool does not appear to be related to either its size or construction material, provided its relative proportions exactly match those of the Great Pyramid. The pyramid's power is maximized when it is oriented with one side accurately aligned to one of the four cardinal points of the compass; however, important empowering results can still occur in the absence of such an alignment.

Although numerous empowerment procedures incorporating the pyramid as a psychic tool have been developed, the empowering benefits of the pyramid sometimes appear to be the result of its presence alone. In group situations, the presence of a pyramid seems to stimulate positive and productive social interaction. In an experimental brainstorming session, for instance, the number and quality of new ideas rapidly increased when a small pyramid of glass was introduced. Along another line, the therapeutic effects of the pyramid were illustrated by a businessman who was encumbered by fear of flying. He overcame the fear by carrying on-board a small, alabaster, pyramid paperweight in his jacket pocket.

Some of the pyramid's benefits could result from an expectancy effect, the belief in the pyramid as an empowering tool; however, significant empowering results have been noted even when the pyramid's presence was unknown. A young woman, for instance, reported a dramatic increase in her husband's sexual prowess when she secretly placed a small cardboard pyramid under his bed. Along a different line, a high school science instructor noted a remarkable increase in student participation, as well as significant improvements in test performance, when he secretly placed a pyramid in the classroom's storage area.

There is an emerging body of evidence to suggest that the pyramid may have important health and fitness applications. In a stop-smoking project, experimental subjects who placed a small cardboard pyramid under their beds were significantly more successful in breaking the smoking habit than control subjects who did not use the pyramid. In another vein, participants in a weight-management program were more successful in achieving their weight-loss goals when a small plastic pyramid was introduced into their group sessions. Our clinical studies showed that the pyramid, when present in group-therapy sessions, promoted relaxation, and more positive group interactions.

Observations of the human aura reveal significant changes in aura patterns and colors when the hands are held briefly over the pyramid. The aura typically expands, its energy patterns become more harmonious, and its colors become increasingly bright. The immediate energizing effects are usually experienced as warm, tingling sensations in the hands.

The pyramid's empowering influence on the body's immune system was suggested by a study investigating the effect of meditation on the tendency to catch colds and other virus-related infections, during a four-month cold and flu season. Twenty experimental subjects, all college students, participated in weekly group meditation, with a pyramid present in their sessions. Twenty control subjects, also college students, participated in similar weekly meditation sessions over the same period, but without the pyramid. The experimental subjects experienced a significantly lower frequency of colds and other virus infections during the four-month period. A replication of the study with another population of college students showed similar results.

The health and fitness potential of the pyramid was further suggested by a writer, who discovered that her blood pressure decreased when she placed a crystal pyramid on a shelf in her study.

Energizing the Aura

By periodically focusing her attention on the pyramid, while affirming her inner potential for wellness, she empowered her body with a healthy flow of positive, healing energy.

In a remarkable demonstration of pyramid power, a retired teacher, who suffered from arthritis, experienced a dramatic decrease in joint pain and swelling after a pyramid night light, a gift from her son, was placed on a dresser in her bedroom. She described the soft glow of the pyramid as "warm, healing energy" which she readily absorbed into the joints of her body. With the aid of the pyramid, she assumed command of the painful illness that had plagued her for many years. She became progressively more active and full of life. Her feelings of helplessness and frustration were replaced by an empowered mental and physical state, which significantly enriched her life.

The health potential of the pyramid in the medical setting was dramatically illustrated by a heart transplant recipient, who attributed his rapid recovery to the power emitted by a cardboard pyramid. Before the transplant, he placed the pyramid under his bed, where it remained during his recovery. The pyramid, he believed, balanced and energized his body's spontaneous healing mechanisms.

These instances of the empowering effects of the pyramid suggest several important concepts with relevance to health and fitness.

1. The very presence of the pyramid can be empowering, even when its presence is unknown to us.

2. Recognizing and accepting the pyramid's empowering potential augments the effectiveness of this psychic tool.

3. Simply formulating personal goals is empowering, but by relating our goals to the pyramid, we can greatly expand our success potential.

4. Expectations of success magnify the empowering potential of the pyramid as a psychic tool.

5. The empowering effects of the pyramid can be significantly amplified through related imagery and positive affirmation.

Although the pyramid, by its presence alone, can be spontaneously empowering, its effectiveness and range of empowering possibilities are dramatically enlarged by a structured approach, which recognizes the empowering potential of this object.

"Moment of Power" is a strategy based on our capacity to interact with the pyramid and, thereby, energize our inner power potentials to a point of maximum saturation. In this procedure, the pyramid is recognized as a dynamic object of beauty, as well as power. The tangible pyramid is seen as a prototype of a super, cosmic pyramid, with singular design and energy frequencies which are responsive to our inner energy system. The four sides of the pyramid reflect the totality of our being—mental, physical, spiritual, and psychic. The pyramid's apex represents our inner capacity for peak empowerment.

The primary goal of the Moment of Power is empowerment of our health and fitness potential to a level which overflows to energize the total body. The supreme point of overflow is usually experienced as a peak influx of power. That peak moment is sometimes described as the psychic equivalent of sexual orgasm. It builds gradually throughout the procedure, and eventually culminates in an intensely forceful and thrilling power release. The empowering results can be deep and lasting. The five-step procedure requires approximately thirty minutes, and can be practiced as either an individual or group exercise.

MOMENT OF POWER STRATEGY

Step 1 *Preparation.* The essential conditions of this procedure are a relaxed setting and a pyramid oriented at approximately eye level. In the group setting, the pyramid is situated on a table near the center of the group.

Step 2 *Preliminary Affirmation.* While seated comfortably and with the pyramid in full view, breathe slowly and deeply, while gazing at the pyramid. Then affirm:

> *This is my moment of power. My past, present, and future converge at this point in time. This is*

my time, my place, and my destiny. Mentally,
physically, spiritually, and psychically, I am
attuned to the infinite power of the universe.

Step 3   *Power Production.* Close your eyes and envision the
pyramid situated on the table before you. Then imagine its super counterpart: a gigantic crystal pyramid on
a distant cosmic plane, glowing and vibrating with
power. Notice your inner power source, vibrantly
attuned to the crystal pyramid. Sense the pulsation of
inner power, building steadily to its peak.

Step 4   *Power Release.* Envision the distant, crystal pyramid
emitting from its apex a powerful beam of energy,
which penetrates the massive core of the universe. At
that moment, envision a thunderous burst of energy
lighting up the heavens. Notice the simultaneous,
thrilling release of powerful energy within yourself,
illuminating your inner being, and permeating your
physical body. Envision every physical organ bathed in
the glow of health, each system renewed and infused
with vigor, and every cell glistening with bright energy.
Notice the all-consuming ecstasy of the experience.

Step 5   *Resolution.* Once again, envision the giant, crystal
pyramid. Although its mission of power is now complete, the glowing pyramid continues to vibrate with
energy. Your total being resonates with the powerful
pyramid. Your physical systems, now fully infused
with vibrant energy, are balanced and synchronized.

Step 6   *Conclusion.* Open your eyes and, while gazing at the
pyramid before you, affirm:

I am saturated with power. I am fully infused with health and wellness energy. I can renew the empowering effects of this experience by simply envisioning the crystal pyramid on a distant plane, glowing with power.

Following the procedure, a brief period of reflection and introspection can add to the empowering effects. In the group setting, the personal benefits of the experience are discussed, with focus on specific empowering results.

The empowering effects of strategies using the pyramid can be later activated through recalling the experience, envisioning the pyramid, and re-affirming the procedure's empowering effects. Consequently, pyramid procedures typically include post-procedural affirmations, and cues emphasizing imagery of the pyramid. This strategy reflects the power of pyramid concepts, even in the absence of the tangible object itself.

Since an actual pyramid is not always available, a strategy known as "Ascending the Pyramid I" was designed to activate a general state of pyramidal empowerment in the absence of the pyramid. The original procedure involved imagery of a pyramid with ten steps leading to its apex. Each step was inscribed with a word that evoked related empowerment affirmations. Inscriptions in the original procedure included love, forgiveness, peace, faith, choice, change, awareness, knowledge, balance, and empowerment.

"Ascending the Pyramid II" is an adaptation of the original procedure, structured specifically to achieve health and physical fitness goals. This adaptation, like the original procedure, is built around imagery of a pyramid with ten steps, each inscribed with a word which gives rise to related empowering affirmations. Essentially a meditation procedure, Ascending the Pyramid II is initiated by closing the eyes, progressively relaxing the body, and envisioning a pyramid with ten steps leading to its apex. Each step, with its inscription, is then envisioned one by one, beginning at the first step and culminating at the apex, as empowering affirmations are presented.

ASCENDING THE PYRAMID II

Step 1   Insight.

> *Insight is power. Insight and self-understanding increase my potential for a healthy, fulfilled, and empowered life. I will use my powers of insight to enrich my life mentally and physically.*

Step 2   Enrichment.

> *My life is an exciting journey of growth, discovery, and change. I possess within myself a rich and bountiful supply of healthy energy. I am empowered to unleash my inner resources and distribute them as needed. I am empowered to tap into the higher planes of the universe to enrich my life with boundless health and vigor.*

Step 3   Focus.

> *I am focused inwardly and outwardly in my quest for a rich, empowered life. My inner powers constantly interact to keep me centered and balanced. Mentally, physically, spiritually, and psychically, my total being is at equilibrium.*

Step 4   Vitality.

> *I am empowered with health and vigor. My body is constantly revitalizing and renewing itself. My immune and defense systems are fortified and empowered to keep me healthy and physically fit.*

Step 5   Rejuvenation.

> *My potential for rejuvenation is strong and enduring. Youthful energy is flowing throughout my total being. The vital organs, systems, and functions of my body are constantly energized and rejuvenated.*

Step 6   Wellness.

> *Each day, I am becoming healthier and more full of energy. Wellness energies are being constantly unleashed to fortify every cell and fiber of my body. Empowered with abundant wellness energy, I am at my best.*

Step 7   Oneness.

> *I am an elegantly designed creation, made of many parts constantly working together as one. My body, mind, and spirit are a smoothly functioning unit, perfectly organized in an intricate framework. I am at one and at peace with myself and the universe.*

Step 8   Intervention.

> *I am empowered to intervene as needed to pro-
> mote my mental and physical well-being. I am
> empowered to banish threats to my health and
> replace them with the positive energies of well-
> ness. All my inner resources and the unlimited
> powers of the universe are at my command.*

Step 9   Attunement.

> *The complex parts of my being are a symphony
> of beauty and perfection. I am an efficient, har-
> monious energy system. I am attuned to the
> inner universe of my being and to the outer uni-
> verse of unlimited power.*

Step 10   Empowerment.

> *In my capacity to be more aware of my body and
> its needs, to enrich my life with healthy energy, to
> maintain mental and physical stability, to
> become infused with vitality, to activate and dis-
> tribute rejuvenating energies, to promote well-
> ness, to experience oneness and peace with
> myself and the universe, to intervene into my
> physical system as needed, and to achieve a state
> of healthy attunement, both inwardly and out-
> wardly, I am fully empowered with abundant
> health and fitness.*

As your eyes remain closed, envision yourself pausing at
the pyramid's apex, your hands, like powerful antennae,

reaching upward toward the higher planes of the universe. Allow your body to become even more empowered with positive energy. Ascending the Pyramid II is concluded with the simple affirmation:

I am empowered.

The Quartz Crystal

The quartz crystal is important as a psychic tool because of its singular properties, often considered to be spontaneously empowering, and its unique amenability to structured empowerment strategies. Apart from its health and fitness applications, the quartz crystal can be incorporated into a wide range of procedures related to other personal goals, including academic and career success.

Spontaneous empowering effects are often more pronounced when the crystal comes to us as a gift. A pre-law student found that a quartz-crystal pendant, a gift from her grandmother, empowered her with increased self-confidence and security. She discovered that she was at her academic best when wearing the pendant necklace. Upon her grandmother's death, the pendant became an important manifestation of her grandmother's empowering presence in her life. Today, she partly attributes her success as a trial attorney to her grandmother's gift, which empowered her as a student, and continues to empower her professional life. "The crystal pendant," she asserts, "is a symbol of my destiny for success."

The crystal as an empowerment tool is particularly conducive to strategies requiring imagery and affirmation. In addition to its usefulness as a point of focus for many meditation approaches, it is a highly effective hypnotic induction tool, when used as a pendulum object. Since the crystal can be carried in the pocket or worn as jewelry, it is also useful as a post-hypnotic or post-meditation tool.

Affirmations presented during hypnosis or meditation can be later activated by simply viewing or touching the crystal.

The crystal has been particularly empowering as a post-hypnotic cue in weight-management programs using self-hypnosis. Examples of workable post-hypnotic suggestions are:

> *I will be in instant control of my appetite by simply stroking the crystal. The crystal is a reminder that I am succeeding. The crystal represents my determination to achieve my goal.*

Similarly, smoking cessation through self-hypnosis can be enhanced by post-hypnotic suggestions such as:

> *By stroking the crystal, I will seal my determination to quit smoking. The crystal is a reminder that I am now a non-smoker. It symbolizes a healthy body and lungs that are clear of toxins.*

At times, the crystal almost seems to have a consciousness of its own. It can show up when needed and disappear when its work is finished, possibly for the purpose of moving on to help someone else in need. A college professor, whose teen-age son had died of leukemia, found a small quartz crystal partly hidden in the carpet of his office. Upon picking up the crystal, he experienced a wondrous surge of serenity and peace of mind. For the first time since his son's death, he felt a calm release of his grief. He valued the crystal as a manifestation of his son's successful transition and enriched existence on the other side.

The quartz crystal is often seen as a trusted helper or friend, rather than simply a tangible object or empowerment tool. An engineer undergoing treatment for cancer noticed a crystal which had mysteriously appeared in a tray among his cuff-links. He was instantly attracted to the object. The crystal became a valued source of comfort throughout his illness. He conceded, "I began to think of the crystal as a faithful friend who shared my pain and helped me to recover." Upon completion of his successful treatment, the crystal vanished as inexplicably as it had appeared, perhaps to pursue another mission of mercy.

The spontaneous appearance of the crystal is sometimes believed to signify an angelic presence. A college student, whose father had recently been killed in an automobile accident, was given a crystal by a stranger whom she took to be another student. The crystal, which she wore as a pendant, became, not only a reminder of a stranger's kindness, but a source of comfort at a time of deep grief. The crystal eventually came to represent the protective presence of a guardian angel, and she wondered whether it had been an angel who had lovingly given it to her.

Although the crystal seems to be strongly empowering at a personal level, there is evidence to suggest that it can have energizing effects on a larger scale. That possibility was illustrated by a crystal mysteriously appearing on the desk of a psychology professor who had recently introduced a fledgling parapsychology program at a small southern college. The appearance of the unique crystal, which encased a perfectly formed pyramid, signaled a period of rapid growth for the program. The program received an important research grant, and acquired a laboratory facility. Interest and enrollment in the program steadily increased, additional research grants were forthcoming, new parapsychology courses were introduced, and a parapsychology endowment fund was established. The crystal, with its unique pyramid, remained on the professor's desk, while the program grew as if energized by it. Finally, with the program firmly established, the quartz crystal mysteriously vanished. The program continued to flourish and, several years later, a report by the regional accreditation agency for colleges and universities recognized the parapsychology program as one of the college's major strengths.

Frequently, a given crystal will mysteriously reappear in our lives from time to time. Shortly after affiliating with a law firm, an attorney discovered a quartz crystal in his office bookcase. He felt an instant affinity for the crystal, characterized by a distinguishing rainbow among its other unusual interior patterns. He placed the crystal on an office credenza, where it remained in full view, until it mysteriously disappeared several months later. The attorney, assuming that the crystal had simply been removed by someone for one reason or another, dismissed the event as inconsequential. A few years later, the highly successful attorney joined a larger organization in a distant city. Upon entering his new office, a quartz crystal on the credenza behind his desk, immediately commanded his attention. He examined the crystal and, to his astonishment, found it to be the same crystal which had previously entered his life. He took the reappearance of the crystal as a good omen—the affirmation of a wise career move, and a prediction of continued professional success. The prominent attorney reports that the crystal, unquestionably working in his behalf, remains with him to this day.

Since the crystal, by its presence alone, is often profoundly empowering, it would follow that its empowering potential could be expanded, and perhaps even redirected, through our deliberate involvement with it. Consequently, the crystal has been incorporated into several step-by-step procedures, which recognize its empowering potential.

Critical to all crystal empowerment strategies is a recognition and appreciation of the crystal as more than simply a tangible, impersonal object. A positive regard for the crystal as an energizing force consistently enhances its empowering capacities and promotes a more productive interaction with it. Possessive ownership of the crystal, however, even when the crystal has been purchased, is usually counter-empowering. The crystal belongs to the universe; our associations with it, although intensely meaningful, are transient. Consequently, terms such as "my crystal," or "our crystal," are not recommended in the empowerment applications of this highly receptive, but independent tool.

"Crystal Interactive Programming" is a step-by-step procedure, in which we interact with the crystal to achieve specifically formulated empowerment goals. The procedure does not attempt to program the crystal as simply a tangible object that awaits our command, nor as a material tool to function in ways we designate. Rather, the crystal is viewed as an equal partner in an empowering interaction. It should be noted that crystals coming into our lives spontaneously are typically pre-programmed for a specific empowerment purpose and, therefore, do not require further programming.

The procedure is based on a threefold premise:

1. The quartz crystal and the human mind can independently access and activate potential sources of power.

2. The human mind and the quartz crystal can engage in a cooperative, two-way interaction that programs both to achieve empowerment goals.

3. The results of interactive programming are synergistic; the empowering capacities of both the mind and the crystal are energized and amplified.

Crystal Interactive Programming can be used to achieve a wide range of empowerment goals, but it is particularly applicable to health and fitness objectives. The procedure builds a positive mental state and strengthens the body's defense system, thus making us less susceptible to disease and illness. While crystals of any color can be used for this procedure, the clear crystal is more amenable to interactive programming.

CRYSTAL INTERACTIVE PROGRAMMING

Step 1   *Selecting a Crystal.* Selecting a crystal for interactive programming is, in itself, an interactive process. Select a crystal that you can hold easily in the hand. When selecting from an assortment, look for the crystal that seems right for you. It is often the first crystal you considered, or the one you tend to go back to. Often, a particular crystal will immediately command your attention, or it will seem to call out to you. It is important to note that a crystal you receive as a gift or through some form of spontaneous materialization, may have chosen *you*, typically for a highly specific empowerment purpose.

Step 2   *Program Unloading.* Because they may retain aspects of previous programming, most crystals will require program unloading. This unloading process is sometimes called "cleansing the crystal," a misnomer, since the crystal is not contaminated but simply requires unloading. To unload an existing program, run cool water over the crystal for approximately one minute, as you hold the crystal in your hand and gently stroke it. Then, place the crystal on a white towel to air dry.

There are other equally effective ways of unloading the crystal. Some of them involve complicated procedures such as burying the crystal for a given period, or leaving it overnight in the moonlight.

Step 3   *Interactive Conditioning.* A positive interaction with the crystal is an essential prerequisite to program loading. First, examine the crystal, noting its particular features— size, shape, and special characteristics. Then, while gently holding the crystal in the cupped palm of either hand, note sensations such as weight and temperature. Pay particular attention to impressions of energy and frequency patterns. Focus on the interaction of your own energies with those of the crystal. Allow the energies to merge and interact. You may experience a satisfying sense of bonding with the crystal.

Step 4 *Program Loading.* Programming the crystal, like the selecting and conditioning process, is interactive. As the crystal continues to rest in the cupped palm of the hand, envision your inner core actively generating powerful energy which interacts with the energies of the crystal. Allow the interaction to build as the energies of your own system, and those of the crystal, become calibrated, resulting in a smooth, continuous flow of energy. You are now ready for a two-way program loading.

As you program the crystal, you are also programming yourself to achieve your health and fitness goals. Mentally formulate your goals, and state them as positive affirmations, employing powerful words and related imagery. Energize your health goals by envisioning the desired end results—a healthier, stronger body, organs functioning smoothly, a body free of toxins and glowing with health, and physical systems revitalized with energy. Engage an empowering interaction with the crystal, as you sense the crystal's acceptance of your goals. Acknowledge the crystal as your partner in a joint endeavor. Focus on the crystal and affirm:

Together, we will achieve these goals.

Step 5 *Program Testing.* As the crystal continues to rest in your hand, notice your own energy system interacting with it. You will sense the building of energy in the crystal

Programming the Crystal

and throughout your body. Envision specific organs and functions, then mentally infuse them with positive energy, until they glow with health. Note the powerful supply of energy at your disposal. You will sense the empowering interaction as it occurs, often as flowing warmth or smooth vibrations of energy. You will notice that dispersing energy actually builds more energy.

Step 6   *Saving the Program.* You can save the empowering program now loaded in the crystal and within yourself by again focusing on your interaction with the crystal and simply affirming:

Please stay.

> The interactive programming now complete, the empowering functions will remain activated, even in the absence of the crystal; however, keeping the crystal close at hand facilitates a continuous interaction, while increasing its empowering capacity. Ideally, the crystal will remain in close proximity to the body, either carried in a pocket or worn as an ornament.

Aside from its usefulness in health and fitness, Crystal Interactive Programming is applicable to many other personal-empowerment goals. In athletics, the procedure has been used effectively to build self-confidence and guide the athlete through a smooth, clean performance. A diving competitor discovered that Crystal Interactive Programming accelerated his mastery of complicated diving skills. In sports such as archery, tennis, and golf, the procedure significantly improved motor coordination and accuracy.

Crystal Interactive Programming is particularly applicable to self-empowerment goals including managing weight, stopping smoking, reducing anxiety and negative stress, overcoming depression, and improving concentration and memory skills. For many of these applications, the crystal is worn as a pendant, typically under the clothing.

CONCEPTUAL GATEWAY TOOLS

Tangible objects, as psychic tools, typically engage some form of imagery or visualization, accompanied by empowering affirmations. As we have seen, after practicing with the object, images of the object itself, called replacement imagery, can evoke significant empowering effects. An example of this phenomenon is pyramidal meditation, where imagery of the pyramid replaces the tangible object. The empowering effects of replacement imagery could be explained as the result of conditioning or association, in which we mentally, and possibly physically, associate a given object with certain empowering consequences. On the other hand, such effects could result from the inherent power of the object itself, which is activated through imagery of it.

Strong empowering results have been demonstrated using strategies which, from the start, substituted conceptual imagery for the tangible object. In these procedures, the focus remains on the object, now absent as a tangible article, but present as a conceptual tool. The power of conceptual imagery suggests that many tangible concepts spontaneously evoke imagery with empowering potential.

The subconscious is particularly responsive to creative imagery of tangibles holding universal significance. Within the subconscious, the collective growth experiences gathered through the centuries are organized around core concepts, often involving tangible objects. These concepts are powerful generators of energy, and if tapped into, provide a gateway to the hidden powers within the self and the outer universe. Given conceptual imagery, we have the essential tool to access those powers.

The "majestic crown" is a universal symbol of power. It typically evokes imagery of powerful monarchs, magical castles, and magnificent kingdoms. Psychically, it symbolizes the regal power within ourselves, and our capacity to engage the highest kingdoms of the universe. The "Crown of Power" incorporates imagery of the crown into a strategy designed as a gateway to the inner and outer sources of power. Although formulated specifically for health and rejuvenation, the procedure can be adapted to any personal-empowerment goal.

Crown of Power Procedure

To begin the procedure, settle back and fully relax your body. With your eyes closed, imagine your inner being as a vast, magnificent kingdom, surrounded by a great wall with immense gates. Envision yourself approaching the massive gates, and opening them with a light touch of your hand. As you step inside, envision yourself instantly enveloped in a glow of radiant energy. Take a few moments to absorb the peace and serenity of your surroundings.

Picture before you an exquisite palace of marble, glistening in the light. Its doors are magnificently carved, and its roof is a towering crystal dome. Upon approaching the palace, you stand in amazement of its resplendent beauty. A touch of your hand is sufficient to open its doors upon even greater splendor. As you step inside, you are enveloped and energized with radiant light streaming from the dazzling crystal dome.

Envision in the center of the expansive room, a marble pedestal, upon which rests a magnificent, bejeweled crown bathed in light from the crystal dome. You are inexorably drawn to the crown, aware that it is your link to the power within yourself, and to the limitless power of the universe.

Envision yourself standing before the pedestal, then reaching forth to touch the crown—the touch that penetrates the infinite power of the universe. The instant outpouring of healthy, rejuvenating energy is all-consuming. The overflow of power permeates your total being.

Envision yourself calmly lifting the exquisite crown and placing it upon your head. The infusion of powerful energy is again immediate and intense. You can, at this moment, have your heart's desire—wisdom, health, happiness, wealth, success—all of these and more.

Crown of Power Touch

Whatever you affirm at this moment is your destiny. Success, peace of mind, rejuvenation, and abundant wellness are now yours. Endless possibilities surround you. Unlimited potential exists within you, awaiting your command to empower and enrich your life. You are the master of your destiny. Your total being—mind, body, and spirit—is fully energized and empowered.

As you remove the crown and return it to its place on the pedestal, the infusion of power continues uninterrupted. Upon leaving the palace, you remind yourself that you can return to it at will, to explore the vastness of its empowering resources. With the kingdom now behind you, you are aware that it belongs to you; it is your inner universe of unlimited power.

A simple technique, called "Crown of Power Touch." can be used to re-activate the empowering effects of this procedure. The technique consists of lifting your hands and touching the area of your forehead that supported the envisioned crown. This symbolic gesture of the bountiful power within your reach requires only seconds, and can be used almost anywhere.

The tools of psychic empowerment offer important new options and strategies for developing our empowerment potentials. They open the power channels of the mind, and they probe the highest energies of the universe. They provide tangible manifestations of our empowerment goals, and they respond to our empowerment strivings. They can be applied to empower the body with health and fitness, and the mind with peace and meaning. Perhaps more importantly, they significantly expand our awareness of our ourselves, and the nature of our presence within the universe.

8

HIGHER DIMENSIONS
OF POWER

The realm we call this physical reality is only one of many dimensions. Our presence on this tangible plane neither precludes the existence of intangible realities nor limits our capacity to interact with them. In fact, some of our most profound experiences involve personal encounters with ethereal dimensions. A fundamental human need is to know the inner-self while, at the same time, stretching our limits for insight and greater knowledge of the higher planes of the universe. Full self-understanding demands awareness on a larger scale—a riveting probe of the inner and outer realities of our existence.

The co-existence of tangible and intangible planes suggests profound empowerment possibilities. At a personal level, our existence as human beings can be seen as a merging of our tangible and intangible parts. The intangible self continuously interacts with the tangible environment, including the physical body and the world around us. This ongoing interaction is of central importance to our physical and mental well-being. In psychic empowerment, a major focus is on the interactions between the mind and the body. As we have seen, numerous psychic strategies have been developed specifically to promote an empowered mind-body relationship.

The internal interactions between the mind and the body are accompanied by a larger interaction between the self and the physical dimension in which we live. Common examples are our social relationships and our physical interactions with our surroundings. The simple act of breathing is an example of the critical interactions we continuously experience with our physical environment.

Among our most empowering interactions are those which engage higher dimensions of reality. Through vehicles such as introspection, meditation, and various altered states, we can probe the highest planes of enlightenment and power. These interdimensional experiences can lift consciousness to new levels, and empower us both mentally and physically. A principal goal of psychic empowerment is the positive engagement of higher dimensions of power.

Occasionally, higher intangible dimensions will merge with tangible planes to produce an extraordinary energy manifestation. Examples are psychic or spiritual healings, the supernatural properties of certain physical settings, and various discarnate phenomena, including ghosts and hauntings. Although these manifestations are often spontaneous and transient, their empowering effects can be intense and enduring.

The merging of tangible and intangible planes occasionally generates visible phenomena, with profound health implications. The site of one such manifestation of power was a stately Greek-Revival mansion, erected on a northern Alabama college campus at the turn of the century. It first served as a residence for the institution's president, then later, as an infirmary, and finally, as a dormitory. Eventually falling into disrepair, the building was abandoned in early 1970, and soon after, the unusual manifestations began. The extraordinary phenomenon consisted of a recurring spherical, green image, seen at night in a second floor window that opened onto the building's front balcony.

Following scores of reported sightings, a group of students enrolled in a parapsychology research course at the college arranged a controlled investigation of the phenomenon. Equipped with photographic and thermal recording equipment, the research team assembled at night in the room where the glowing image had reportedly appeared. The investigative situation consisted of a center table around which the group of sixteen students was seated in a circular arrangement. A candle at the center of the table provided the only available lighting.

An astonishing series of events unfolded in the session that followed. Within minutes, the room's temperature dropped from a Fahrenheit reading of seventy-six degrees to sixty-seven degrees. The lighted candle extinguished itself, and a green spherical glow, approximately fourteen inches in diameter, suddenly appeared over the table, where it remained for the duration of the hour-long session. Periodic temperature probes of the glow revealed Fahrenheit readings ranging from eighty-six to eighty-nine degrees, while the surrounding room temperature remained around sixty-seven degrees.

During the appearance of the green glow, a pre-med student, who had recently sustained a wrist injury, thrust her hand and swollen wrist into the green form, and experienced, in her words, "a vibrant, healing warmth." The pain immediately ceased, and by the session's end, her wrist had returned to normal. Each participant on the team touched the glowing image and, without exception, experienced warm, tingling vibrations. Attempts to photograph the image were, unfortunately, unsuccessful.

In a series of subsequent evening sessions, the spherical glow consistently appeared, uncovering an extensive range of amazing health possibilities. A faculty member suffering from arthritis experienced instant relief from pain, and progressive improvement, following a single session in which he briefly held his hands in the spherical glow. An athlete successfully transferred energy from the green image to his injured knee, by first holding his hands in the glow, and then massaging his swollen knee. The pain, he reported, ceased instantly, and by the following day, the swelling was gone. A student suffering chronic back pain resulting from an automobile injury found that, by simply holding his hands in the sphere of energy, he could reduce the pain. He practiced the procedure, which we called "spherical therapy," twice weekly over a period of two weeks. With each session, the pain diminished; by the fourth session, it had ceased.

Research of the extraordinary phenomenon, including unsuccessful efforts to encapsulate and preserve the energy, continued over several months. Eventually, the building underwent extensive renovation, during which the stately mansion was severely altered, rather than restored. The building's painted-brick exterior was chemically stripped, and its original windows, doors, and woodwork were replaced. Its ceilings were lowered, partitions were removed, and drywalls were installed. Its exquisite, antique chandeliers were replaced with fluorescent lights, and its hardwood floors were covered with commercial, wall-to-wall carpet. Sadly, the reckless onslaught on the historic building was so traumatic that the energy manifestations abruptly ceased. With its splendid ambiance gone, the formerly stately structure became known as "the building that lost it soul."

Empowering interactions between tangible and intangible dimensions are often so finely tuned that even minor alterations can disrupt or totally extinguish the delicate phenomena. When we disregard the positive powers of higher dimensions, or when we irresponsibly intervene into the manifestations of those powers, we thwart their capacity to empower and enrich our lives. An appreciation of higher sources of power, and a keen awareness of our ability to interact with them, are essential conditions for optimizing our personal empowerment potentials.

The psychic-empowerment model of health and fitness, while emphasizing the positive aspects of the self and other planes, recognizes the potentially disempowering sides of both. Disempowering conditions can result from either the accumulation of oppressive energies over time, or the enfeebling influences of lower planes.

Occasionally, anomalous manifestations of energy are negatively centered in tangible settings, from residential to high-rise structures. A southern college dormitory, later to serve as a faculty office building, was the site of an apparent accumulation of negative energy, first reported by its student residents. The earliest reported manifestations were recurring instances of grating sounds, and a dark apparition wandering the building's second floor halls, typically late at night.

During a five-year period in which the building was vacant, the manifestations apparently ceased; however, they resumed with intensity following the building's renovation for use as faculty offices. The apparitions and grating sounds were accompanied by drafts and musty odors. As the manifestations intensified, a faculty assistant was so distressed by the reoccurring phenomena that she asked to be transferred to another building. A psychology professor, working late into the night at his desk, experienced first a draft, then an uneasy awareness of an invisible presence, just before it materialized as a gray apparition in the doorway behind him. He was so shaken by the experience, that he hung a mirror over his desk, which faced a wall, to provide a rear view of the room and, hopefully, advance warning of any intruder.

These unexplained manifestations, though at times unsettling, were first seen as mostly harmless or even amusing; however, a darker side of the phenomenon soon emerged. The manifestations became more frequent and increasingly unnerving, with some chilling, negative overtones. With only a few exceptions, the people who occupied the building developed health problems or significant mental distress, if only for relatively brief periods. Environmental measurements, including tests for asbestos and chemical toxicity, ruled out the presence of environmental hazards. The evolving situation prompted a review of the building's earlier history, which uncovered an unusually high incidence of illness and accidents involving former residents of the building, when it was a dormitory. Taken together, the building's history and existing manifestations suggested a negative influence at work, along with the possibility of an accumulation of toxic energy. Although numerous corrective procedures are available to banish such negative influences, their empowerment potential is not always recognized, as was, unfortunately, the case in this situation. Consequently, corrective procedures were not undertaken, and the disempowering manifestations continued unabated.

In the absence of corrective intervention, chronically disempowering, tangible settings can continue to generate a negative force, with serious, cumulative effects. Prolonged exposure to ongoing, negative interactions, and the resulting accumulation of toxic energy, can exact a heavy toll on both mind and body. Like stress, the wear and tear effects of negative energy can disempower us mentally and physically. Admittedly, to attribute adverse mental and physical reactions to a tangible setting and its disempowering manifestations, rather than to conventionally accepted causative factors, requires a quantum leap. Often supporting such a leap, however, is the body of convincing evidence, along with the frequent absence of any other known explanation for such adverse reactions.

A striking instance of an apparent disempowering interaction involved a university professor who developed serious symptoms of illness soon after moving into a house built around 1970. She discovered that her unusual symptoms, while not responding to conventional treatment, disappeared during protracted absences from the house, only to recur when she returned. Suspecting that the residence could the source of her symptoms, she contacted former occupants and found, to her amazement, that the women experienced her exact symptoms, but only while living in the house. Inexplicably, the male residents and the children were unaffected. Numerous environmental tests of the house and its surroundings yielded no explanation for her unusual symptoms.

Suspecting an intangible influence at work, she engaged psychically trained specialists, who cleared the house of negative influences, and reprogrammed it with empowering, positive energy. Following the procedure, her condition progressively improved, and eventually, she became free of all symptoms.

The energies which characterize a building are often present immediately upon its construction, and in some instances, even before construction is complete. The impressions we experience upon entering a building are, in part, a function of the mental and physical energies vested in it. The amount of time, and the nature of human energy expended in its construction, become integral parts of the finished building. In that sense, the completed structure becomes a programmed entity—the sum of the energy that went into it. This concept could help explain the extraordinary powers of the Great Pyramid. The structure's existence attests to the mastery of its design, and to the enormous energies required to build it.

From inception to completion, buildings are programmed, in part at least, by human input. Following a building's construction, the input and programming continues. Although the influence of other dimensions can be critical to the programming process, the ongoing human interactions associated with a structure can energize it further, with either positive or negative power. When the programming is disempowering, unloading the negative and reloading with the positive is essential.

When moving into a new workplace or residence, appropriate clearing and reprogramming can extinguish disempowering influences, and charge the setting with positive energy which is mentally and physically empowering. "Environmental Clearing and Reprogramming" is a procedure structured first, to intervene into disempowering interactions and dismantle them, and second, to banish negative influences and replace them with empowering energy. This highly positive strategy is applicable to any physical setting—industrial, commercial, political, religious, or residential. The procedure is typically implemented on-site, or as close as possible to the physical setting

ENVIRONMENTAL CLEARING AND REPROGRAMMING

Step 1   Prior to entering the situation to be cleared and reprogrammed, engage imagery of pure, white energy, enveloping your total being. Mentally erect a sphere of positive energy around you, and affirm:

> *I am empowered with positive, radiant energy.*
> *I am protected and secure. I am attuned to the*
> *highest power of the universe. I can draw from*
> *that source at any moment to empower myself,*
> *and to energize my surroundings. I am filled and*
> *overflowing with powerful, positive energy.*

Step 2   Upon entering the area to be cleared and reprogrammed, envision a channel of pure light connecting you and your surrounding sphere of energy to the bountiful energies of universe. Picture the highest power of the universe as radiant light, abundantly energizing yourself and your surroundings. Envision the darkness of your surroundings giving way to the radiant light.

Step 3   Move slowly throughout the area of clearing and reprogramming, pausing wherever needed, as you affirm:

> *I am a channel of light and positive power. The infinite power of the universe is now available to me. All the negative energies around me are now neutralized and replaced with the light of positive energy. This place is now fully energized with peace and radiant light. The positive powers of the universe will remain in this place, to permeate it with light and healthy energy.*

Another strategy, the "Psychic Protection Procedure," is used in personal empowerment to neutralize and release disempowering forces surrounding the self, while offering protection from residual effects or further invasion of negative energy. The procedure replenishes our positive energy supply, and prevents further depletion of our energy system. The Psychic Protection Procedure is not an environmental clearing or reprogramming procedure. It is designed for personal empowerment only; however, it is often used before and after environmental clearing and reprogramming efforts.

PSYCHIC PROTECTION PROCEDURE

Step 1   Envision a higher dimension of pure, white light, and a channel of energy connecting you to it. Imagine positive energy streaming into your being and enveloping your body with a sparkling, radiant shield of power. Affirm:

I am fully enveloped and infused with positive energy. I am empowered to repel the onslaught of negative forces. I am fully empowered in mind and body.

Step 2 Bring the fingers of both hands together in a praying hands position, to balance your energy system. Affirm:

The systems of my being are in perfect harmony. I am saturated mentally and physically with positive energy.

Step 3 Conclude the procedure by joining the tips of your thumb and middle finger of each hand, then bringing them together to form interlocking circles, a gesture which protects your energy supply. Affirm:

I am at my peak of mental and physical empowerment. I am protected and secure.

INTERACTIONS WITH DISCARNATE DIMENSIONS

The survival of consciousness after death, and our capacity to interact with discarnate planes, suggest profound empowerment possibilities. Spontaneously sensing the presence of a departed loved one, for instance, can be a source of comfort and peace, not only for the survivor, but for the departed as well. The need to interact is basic to both temporal and non-temporal dimensions of consciousness.

Unfortunately, the transition process is thwarted at times, and the resulting interaction takes on disempowering properties. Several conditions can contribute to such disempowering phenomena. A traumatic, untimely death can result in a difficult transition, because of resistance on the part of both the deceased and the survivors. Unresolved conflict, remorse, and fear can bind the departed to this plane, and arrest growth on the other side. Faulty relationships, inadequate personality patterns, and unfulfilled strivings, particularly unrequited love, can likewise impede progress, not only in the after-life, but on this plane as well.

Entities whose discarnate progress is thwarted, are believed, at times, to engage the energy systems of others on this plane in disempowering interactions. Suspended between dimensions and not attuned to the higher plane called light, they may turn to the temporal dimension as an energy source. Like the temporal "psychic vampire," the "discarnate vampire" psychically taps into the energy supply of persons on this plane. The results are a temporary replenishment of energy for the discarnate entity, and a depletion of energy for the temporal host, a price some host victims appear willing to pay. Such a relationship can become co-dependent, with both the survivor and deceased locked into a dependency interaction which is self-perpetuating, although typically not fully understood by either. The long-term effect is disempowerment for all involved. These disempowering interactions can usually be resolved by loosening the dependency bond through such strategies as the Psychic Protection Procedure.

The seance and table-tilting are sometimes used to access discarnate dimensions, and explore the interactions between dimensions. These techniques, when appropriately applied, can gain pertinent information regarding unexplained manifestations, and promote healthy, empowering interactions. Both procedures are based on the premise that personal, conscious identity and growth continue in the discarnate or after-death state. Discarnate manifestations are seen as meaningful, although not always empowering, interactions between the discarnate plane and the temporal dimension. Such manifestations are frequently a call for help from the other side. Although table-tilting and the seance are designed primarily to promote mutually empowering interactions between dimensions, they can be applied specifically to liberate earth-bound entities who may be locked in the transition process, or whose progress on the other side is otherwise thwarted. These empowering procedures can also provide critical information regarding life after death, as well as the nature of interactions between temporal and non-temporal dimensions. It is important to note that table tilting and the seance are advanced procedures, and they should be practiced only with appropriate orientation and training.

The role of discarnate dimensions in health and fitness is one of the most challenging areas of psychic empowerment. There exists a growing body of evidence to suggest that positive interactions, whether within the self, with others, or with a higher plane, promote better mental and physical health. This was illustrated by a college student whose reaction to the sudden, untimely death of his father almost destroyed his life. Guilt resulting from an altercation with his father, and conflict concerning his father's untimely death, exacted a serious toll on the student's personal, academic, and social life. His grades plummeted, and over the months, he became increasingly despondent. Drug abuse and serious health problems followed, as his life spun increasingly out-of-control.

Plagued by these adverse circumstances, he was eventually hospitalized, whereupon he experienced an interaction with his deceased father that turned his life around. By his account, he awakened at twilight, to see his father standing beside his hospital bed. As he reached out and took his father's hand, his father said simply, "Son, I love you," then faded into the light. At that moment, the student experienced a thrilling surge of positive energy, and a full release of his grief and guilt. The riveting interaction was a critical turning-point in his life. His health rapidly improved, and he took command of his life again. He successfully resumed his undergraduate studies, and completed a graduate program. Today, an eminent attorney, he attributes his survival and success to the unforgettable interaction with his deceased father. "It was not a dream," he asserts. "It was a visit from the other side."

EMPOWERING INTERACTIONS WITH NATURE

Our natural surroundings provide optimal conditions for empowering experiences with higher planes. Nature offers a tangible manifestation of the endless power of the universe. Through our interactions with nature, we can access that unlimited power source. Not surprisingly, some of our most profoundly empowering and unforgettable peak experiences involve interactions with nature. Mentally and physically, most of us are empowered by a spectacular sunset, bathing the earth with beauty and inspiring the spirit to soar. Likewise, a thrilling rainstorm sweeping across the plains, revitalizing the earth and stirring the soul, or a winter snow-storm quietly blanketing the earth and gently soothing the heart, are both part of the empowering grandeur of the greater universe. We can scarcely comprehend its splendor and illimitable power. When we are attuned to that power, we are at our physical, mental, and spiritual peak.

Health issues which involve delicate biochemical processes are particularly responsive to interactions with the instruments of nature. The biological and psychological components of depression, for instance, are highly responsive to nature's healing balm. Experiences which inspire the spirit will invariably revitalize the body, whereas experiences which suppress the spirit will invariably enfeeble the body. This was illustrated by a professor who fell into severe depression, which progressively worsened following the death of his companion. He developed serious health problems, and eventually lost his will to live. At the depths of his despair, he left his office early on a winter afternoon to drive into the mountains alone. As he drove along a winding road, a gathering of blackbirds perched on the road's guardrail strangely commanded his attention. Perfectly spaced on the rail, the birds remained motionless as he slowly approached them. Marveling at their shining beauty, he noticed, to his amazement, an incredibly radiant white bird—but apparently of the same species—perched among the others. Suddenly, the white bird took flight, leaving the others transfixed in their perch on the rail. The professor pulled to the roadside and watched the ascending bird, until it finally disappeared from sight. At that moment, he felt his grief being gently lifted, and replaced by wondrous peace. He thought of his companion, not as tragically departed into the dark unknown, but rather as joyfully ascended into the light of a higher, more beautiful dimension of enriched existence. Empowered mentally and physically by the simple but unforgettable peak experience, he shifted his life forward with renewed purpose and hope. His health and career again flourished. In his words, "The experience is a treasured gift. I will never forget it."

Many natural settings are uniquely energized with empowering potentials. These special places can be a personal hideaway, where we go for physical and mental renewal, or they can be special retreats where we gather as groups for self-empowerment or to advance global causes, such as promoting world peace, saving our dying oceans, or raising global consciousness. These energized retreats can empower individuals and groups with inspiration, purpose, and commitment. Moreover, they provide opportunities for us to amass our energies, and focus them to achieve important goals and bring forth change on the planet.

At a deeply personal level, many of us have discovered a special place where our empowering potential seems to be at its peak. A uniquely energized sanctuary, for instance, can stir the spirit and lift awareness to new levels. Mentally and physically, almost everyone is empowered by returning to an old homeplace, with its treasure of memories. Going back to the past, if only in memory, can inspire and empower us, particularly in times of trial, to face the future and press forward with renewed hope and purpose.

One of our most empowering resources is the primeval forest, with its giant trees, lush undergrowth, rushing streams, and verdant floor teeming with life. Every inch of the forest is a celebration of abundance and joy. The sounds of renewal reverberate like an anthem under its vaulting canopy of leaves. It is a powerful convergence of the highest energies of nature. By simply walking through it, we are able to draw from this powerful repository of healing energy. Contemplating its beauty and absorbing its serenity are empowering to the mind, body, and spirit.

Throughout history, the rugged tree, nature's largest tangible manifestation of life, has provided the focal point at which human powers merged to shape the future. Under the Akenwyke Yew, at Runnymede, England, King John signed the *Magna Carta* in 1215. George Washington took command of the Continental Army under the Cambridge Elm, in Massachusetts, in 1775. Texas declared its independence under the Masonic Charter Oak near Brazoria, Texas, in 1836. These ancient trees became memorials to progress and symbols of freedom and power.

In our personal empowerment, the regal tree can provide the focal point at which we unite with the higher energies of the universe to empower our lives. Since the tree is the biggest plant on earth, and because it is so permanent, we look to it as a unique manifestation of life on a massive scale. In many ways, the design of the tree parallels the complex design of our own physiology. The tree is a smoothly operating system, with each component serving a critical function. Most importantly, throughout its life, it never stops growing. This magnificent antenna of the planet provides the ideal channel for an empowering interaction with higher planes.

The self-empowerment procedure called "Tree Power Interfusion" is based on a twofold premise: first, certain tangible elements of nature, including trees, represent the loftiest planes of the universe; second, our interactions with these elements can open the floodgates of unlimited power. The procedure provides a direct, physical link to universal growth, healing, and wellness energies, as manifested in the majestic tree.

Tree Power Interfusion recognizes not only the symbolic significance of trees, but also their inherent energy attributes and differential empowering effects, depending upon the age and type of tree. Typically, younger trees are associated with flexibility and rejuvenation; older trees signify stability and harmony. Broadleaf trees manifest achievement and abundance; needle-leaf trees represent energy infusion and adaptation. Trees bearing flowers with petals represent creativity and expanded awareness. The oak is an all-purpose tree that is useful for all empowerment goals. The following list illustrates the autonomously empowering characteristics of various types of trees.

Empowering Characteristics of Trees

Beech	Financial success, leadership, and initiative.
Black Walnut	Practicality, independence, and problem-solving.

Cottonwood	Productivity, endurance, and adaptability.
Elm	Conflict resolution, self-understanding, and inner awareness.
Ginkgo	Psychic unfoldment, humanitarian achievements, and universal wisdom.
Hickory	Personal achievement, stability, and self-discipline.
Pine	Abundant energy, immediate fulfillment, and control.
Poplar	Physical health, rejuvenation, and attunement.
White Birch	Spirituality, compassion, and inner peace.

The effectiveness of Tree Power Interfusion depends upon clearly formulated goals and positive affirmations of the expected empowering effects.

TREE POWER INTERFUSION

Step 1   Select a tree, preferably a large one, that appeals to you and seems appropriate for your empowerment goals. Pay particular attention to the stateliness of the tree—its height, shape, and colors.

Step 2   Rest your hands on the tree and note its unique features. Notice particularly the patterns and texture of its bark. Stroke the tree and sense its power. Notice the responsiveness of the tree, as your energies merge with it.

Step 3   With your eyes closed, envision the tree as a giant antenna piercing the unlimited power sources of the universe. As your hands continue to rest on the tree,

Tree Power Interfusion

envision the inner core of your own energy system radiating powerful energy. Allow the energies of your being to interact with the energies of the tree. Notice the physical vibration of that interaction and the infusion of positive energy. Allow the physical infusion to continue until you are overflowing with powerful energy.

Step 4 Present your previously formulated goals and related affirmations.

Step 5   Conclude the infusion process by again stroking the tree, as you mentally express gratitude and recognition of its splendor and power.

The empowering effects of this procedure can be amplified by leaning backward against the tree, and with the back resting against the tree trunk, affirming:

> The energies of my being are balanced and attuned to the powers of this tree and the universe. I am infused with health and vitality. I am fortified with positive growth potential. Mentally, physically, and spiritually, I am empowered.

Tree Power Interfusion has been highly effective as a pain-management procedure. A college student with a long history of tension headaches used the technique with a poplar tree to successfully control the severity and frequency of the headaches. The procedure has also been effective in relieving pain associated with back problems. Reduced stress and increased vitality almost always accompany any application of this procedure.

Aside from its health applications, Tree Power Interfusion is useful as an empowering procedure to build self-esteem, increase motivation, and promote personal success. For these applications, the goal-related affirmations presented in Step Four can focus on activities such as succeeding at a particular task or achieving an important personal or career goal. For goals such as losing weight and stopping smoking, the procedure builds determination and an empowered state of success expectancy.

In addition to the tree, the ocean, mountain peak, and open plain are important natural sources of strength and power. For many of us, these represent our aspirations and the limitless possibilities before us. Occasionally, they evoke memories of the past, with significant empowering results. During hypnosis, a subject with fear of heights was mentally guided up a mountain to its peak, as suggestions of relaxation were presented along the way. Upon reaching the mountain's peak, he experienced a clear flashback of falling from a cliff to his death in a previous life. Given insight into the source of his fear, and armed with the desensitization effects of hypnosis, he was completely liberated from a phobia which had plagued him for many years.

The empowering effects of the sea, that wondrous habitat of bountiful plant and animal life, are often so intense that we are drawn back to it time and time again. An artist, believing she had exhausted her creative potential, found that a visit to the sea energized her physically, and unleashed an abundance of creative power. Upon having visited the sea several times to renew her creative powers, she discovered that simply envisioning the sea was similarly empowering.

The spaciousness of the open plain invites us to stretch our limits and explore other dimensions of our existence. All too often, our thinking becomes constricted, and we lose sight of the opportunities around us. The freedom of the open plain reminds us that our perceived limits are self-imposed; if we look beyond them, we discover a new world of exciting possibilities. We can create change, find solutions, and discover new knowledge. We can take charge of our health, live longer, and get more out of life. We can save the planet, and make it a safer, healthier place for ourselves and our children.

Our existence on this tangible plane is a continuous process of growth and fulfillment. We possess the inner mechanisms which can connect us to the highest dimensions of power. We are surrounded by many tangible manifestations of that wondrous power. We have, at our disposal, an abundance of empowerment tools to promote our progress and ensure our success. Given these resources, we can affirm with certainty:

I am destined for greatness.

* 9 *

ANGELIC INTERACTIONS

In science, we encounter many extraordinary phenomena which cannot be explained by existing principles and theory. These phenomena are observed both inside and outside the laboratory, but they do not easily fit our conventional framework of physical reality. These unexplained events suggest at least two important possibilities: first, crucial knowledge regarding the scientific nature of the universe remains to be discovered; second, many dimensions exist, some of which we know, but many of which we cannot know within the constructs of our current thinking and perspectives. Increasingly, eminent scientists, representing various disciplines, concede the existence of other dimensions beyond our known reality.

In recent years, emerging psychic knowledge has pushed back the borders of science to provide many new ways of perceiving reality and explaining the previously unexplainable. Rather than unraveling the fabric of science, psychic knowledge introduces new designs, principles, and concepts for not only interpreting our existence, but also empowering our lives. The world and the universe are seen in the broader context of greater realities, with many dimensions and planes of power awaiting our further discovery and interaction.

Psychic-empowerment strategies are based upon our capacity to interact with both seen and unseen realities. A wide range of empowering interactions is essential to our growth and survival. We interact with our physical body to achieve health and physical-fitness goals. We interact with the inner self to access and unleash vast inner sources of power. We interact with others to meet our social needs, or to achieve mutually empowering goals. We interact with our natural surroundings to achieve a variety of personal goals. At another level, we interact with higher, non-physical planes to meet our loftier needs for knowledge, insight, and understanding. Through our interactions with the greater universe, we discover unlimited sources of power which give meaning to our existence.

Many of our empowering interactions demand acquired skills to access and activate sources of power which, otherwise, would remain outside our reach. Other empowering phenomena, however, are effortless and spontaneous. They spring voluntarily from within ourselves, or they rise without prompting from our natural surroundings. Invariably, they link awareness to new sources of power, laden with growth potential. Frequently, they involve manifestations of unseen dimensions, which inspire us and enrich our lives with raised consciousness of empowering possibilities.

Among our most highly empowering experiences are our personal interactions with special entities called angels. Typically considered messengers from a higher, unseen dimension, angels are intelligent beings whose interventions into our known reality are always purposeful and empowerment-driven. Even when their presence is not recognized, angels offer vital channels for growth and enrichment. In challenging life situations, they can fortify us with courage and determination. When we face adversity and danger, they offer a splendid shield of protection and assurance. On a physical level, they can infuse us with the bright energies of abundant health and vitality. Finally, at the time of our transition, they can give peace and comfort in our passage from this reality to the discarnate state of continued existence. They assure us that we are not alone in our ascension into the light of the other side. The so-called angel of death is, to the contrary, the angel of light and love. Given the gentle presence of angels, death becomes a wondrous gateway to a higher plane of enriched existence, rather than a fearful leap into the dark. Our psychic-empowerment model for health and fitness would be severely flawed if it omitted the possibility of empowering interactions with angels.

Belief in angels is widespread, and there exists a mounting body of evidence suggesting that human interactions with angels are not infrequent. Angel visitations can involve visible, audible, and other physical manifestations, or they can simply be an expanded awareness of an empowering presence. They can appear in the physical form of a person, or as a supernatural, ghost-like image. They can communicate with us through both sensory and extrasensory channels. Occasionally, their interventions alter situations around us, typically to protect us from harm, or to reassure us of their guiding presence.

Although our interactions with angels often center on common, everyday concerns, they can involve profoundly critical life and death situations. A graduate student experienced an angel visitation which may have prevented his involvement in a serious traffic accident. On the morning of a planned skiing trip, he saw, in his bathroom mirror, a reflection of a glowing figure standing beside him. Although the image was blurred, he immediately recognized it as the angel who had once visited him just hours before he was injured in a motorcycle accident, and again just before his father was injured at a construction site. Interpreting the dramatic visitation as a warning, he canceled his skiing trip. Later that day, the van in which he would have been a passenger skidded out of control and down an embankment. Fortunately, none of the passengers was seriously injured.

In another incident involving danger, a college student, while driving hurriedly to class, felt a hand press firmly against his shoulder as he approached a sharp curve in the road. He immediately applied his brakes, and barely avoided colliding with a truck stalled on a narrow bridge just beyond the curve. The hand, he asserts, was that of his guardian angel, who had communicated with him frequently in the past, typically in situations involving threat or danger. He had come to know the angel as a caring friend who was always present to offer support and protection whenever needed.

Many of our ostensibly psychic experiences could be explained as interactions with angels, rather than products of our psychic faculties alone. Precognitive impressions, particularly of future danger, along with many of our intuitive and clairvoyant insights, often appear to involve angelic revelations. Likewise, it is conceivable that some instances of apparent PK, particularly in critical life and death situations, could instead be the products of angelic interventions. As we develop psychically, we become increasingly attuned and responsive to the presence of angels who interact with us, not only directly, but indirectly through our psychic channels.

Children seem particularly responsive to the benevolent presence of angels. Many children become vividly aware of angels at a very early age, and they often develop rewarding, enduring relationships with their angel friends. Even imaginary angels (typically as playmates) are a positive, healthy part of child development. When such imagery is discouraged, the potential for empowering angelic interactions is severely diminished. Under those constrictions, the normal manifestations of angels become increasingly distant and oblique. Only with maturity and experience do we regain the lost awareness of the empowering presence of angels in our lives.

Our experiences with angels as protectors and guides offer yet another confirmation of our spiritual nature and the endlessness of our conscious existence. Many persons who experience near-death recall the presence of angels who escorted them to the other side, then gently guided them back to this temporal dimension. Similarly, accident and near-accident reports often include descriptions of loving angels who gave protection and guidance at times of peril.

In some instances, angels intervene physically to assume command of emergency situations spinning out of our control. Accompanied by his wife, a college professor was suddenly stricken with a heart-attack while driving on a busy interstate. Unconscious, he slumped over onto his wife, thus preventing her from taking control of the car, as it continued to speed dangerously down the inside lane of the roadway. Then, as if guided by an unseen force, the car promptly crossed the road's three lanes, pulled to the side of the road, and came to a safe stop. Months later, in a public address following his recovery, the formerly agnostic professor concluded his account of the amazing experience with the observation, "The power of angels is possibly the most unrecognized, underrated force in the universe."

Angelic manifestations are often channels of healing for both mind and body. In times of life-threatening illness, the visitation of angels is particularly evident. Lingering in a critical, comatose state following an automobile accident, a college student was visited by an angel, clearly visible to his parents as they watched over their hospitalized son. Suddenly appearing in the middle of the night as a glowing figure at the foot of their son's bed, the angel lingered briefly, radiating light which filled the room. Upon slowly fading away, the angel left behind a radiance visibly enveloping the student throughout the remainder of the night. At dawn, he awoke from the coma and, turning to his parents, remarked with a smile, "You won't believe what happened to me last night. I was visited by an angel." The experience was not only the turning point in his full recovery, it gave new meaning to his existence, and changed his perceptions of life and death.

It is conceivable that the presence of angels is ongoing in everyone's life. Unfortunately, we tend to become aware of angels only under highly extenuating circumstances, or when the angelic intervention is pronounced or uncommonly intense. Awareness of angels, openness to their interventions, and acceptance of their empowering gifts are conditions which consistently promote our mental and physical well-being.

In many ways, angels can be compared to the higher part of the self. Like the higher self, angels are a source of enormous empowering potential, often manifesting itself spontaneously. Furthermore, angels, like the higher self, are constantly poised to respond to our overtures and probes of their empowering potentials; however, they do not impose their resources upon us. Finally, angels, like the higher self, often use dreams as channels for expanding our awareness. A businessperson, whose manufacturing firm was threatened with failure, had a dream in which an angel appeared and unfolded before him a plan which not only saved his company, but initiated an important phase of company growth as well. He recognized the angel as having appeared to him in previous dreams, once following the death of his twin brother, and again when he was faced with the breakup of his marriage. In each instance, the angel gave comfort and reassurance which empowered him to effectively cope with a critical life situation.

At times, angels are known to appear in our dreams for the express purpose of arming us for an impending crises. A photographer experienced recurring dreams, in which a woman took her by the hand and guided her through a burning building to safety. Although she could not identify the smoke-filled building, she recognized the woman as the familiar angel whose picture hung over her bed in childhood. When she was later trapped in a fire on an upper floor of the building where she worked, the familiar angel appeared exactly as in her dreams, and led her by the hand through the smoke to safety before suddenly vanishing.

A psychologist reported recurring dreams in which the car she was driving was struck on the passenger's side by a truck, throwing her car into the path of an approaching vehicle. In each dream, a radiant angel gently assured her, "You are protected." When the accident finally occurred as predicted by her dreams, she sensed the unmistakable presence of the familiar angel, again reassuring her in a soft voice, "You are protected." Although her car was totaled, she escaped the accident unharmed.

Since the presence of angels is typically quiet and unassuming, our willingness to be guided by them or to work with them is essential to their empowering effectiveness. While on a class field trip, two students decided to explore an unfamiliar cave. Unfortunately, the inexperienced spelunkers failed to take essential precautions, and became lost in the cave's labyrinth of passageways. After wandering through the cave for what seemed like hours, they had just stopped to rest, when they heard a distant voice calling, "this way." Although they did not recognize the voice, they followed the repeated calls, which eventually led them safely from the cave. Upon rejoining their classmates, they were amazed to learn that their absence from the group had gone completely unnoticed. There had been no rescue effort. What had seemed like hours in the cave turned out to be less than an hour. Nevertheless, for the two students, the experience was an unforgettable manifestation of a caring presence from another dimension.

EXPANDING AWARENESS OF ANGELS

Invariably, our lives are enriched by expanding our awareness of the possibilities within ourselves as well as those around us. Heightened awareness empowers us to benefit from existing opportunities, while creating new ones. We discover new dimensions within ourselves, and generate new capacities for interacting with higher planes. By increasing our awareness of angels, we become more attuned to the dimensions in which they exist, and more responsive to their empowering influences.

Certain angels appear to remain permanently with us throughout life as personal guides or guardians; others seem to enter our lives temporarily from time to time for specific purposes. We can increase our awareness of their presence and empowering missions in a variety of ways. As already noted, manifestations of angels are particularly common in childhood. By returning to an old homeplace or other site associated with our childhood, we can often evoke early memories of angels, while sharpening our awareness of their continued presence in our lives. The physical settings of early growth are often uniquely energized with the positive influences which protected and guided us through childhood.

Persons who face crises in their lives are often drawn inexplicably to the significant places of their childhood. A teacher, who suffered chronic inflammatory kidney disease, was advised by medical specialists that she would eventually require dialysis or a kidney transplant. Shaken by these unsettling projections, she began to reflect upon her life and search for new meaning. As she reviewed her past, she felt inexorably drawn to her rural birthplace. Upon eventually visiting the rustic setting, she paused under an old maple tree where, as a child, she had spent many carefree hours with an imaginary playmate she had named "Maggie." Reflecting on those happy experiences, she felt the heavy weight of despondency and anxiety begin to lift. She felt anew the wondrous vitality of childhood, as though she had stepped back in time. Lingering under the old tree, she sensed the quiet closeness of Maggie. After a few moments, she brought herself to address the angelic presence, "My dear friend Maggie, thank you for being here."

Leaving the tranquil place behind, she would return to draw strength from it time and time again in the months that followed. With each visit, she became progressively revitalized as her health steadily improved. Perhaps even more importantly, she discovered rich, new meaning to her life. Maggie's presence, no longer confined to the maple tree, increasingly became a constant, energizing force, which empowered her mentally and physically. Her illness slowly reversed itself, and eventually, her health was completely restored. Today, she attributes her recovery to the healing power of a higher dimension revealed to her through her cherished friend, Maggie.

As already indicated, angels are often introduced into our lives during sleep, a state considered to be exceedingly responsive to the influence of higher dimensions. We can facilitate that empowering process through strategies which intervene into the sleep state. A simple, but highly effective technique uses appropriate suggestions presented in the drowsy state just prior to sleep. This strategy will often increase our awareness of angels and their potentially empowering roles in our lives. The following are examples of effective suggestions:

> I am becoming increasingly aware of angels in my life. As I sleep, I will be attuned to their presence and responsive to their messages. I will be energized mentally and physically by their influence. Angels connect me to the highest dimensions of inner and outer power. I welcome and value the presence of angels in my life.

Angels introduced to us during sleep typically appear as familiar beings, but whose identities we do not recognize. They are usually attractive in appearance, and their presence is invariably comforting and inspiring. Only by coming to know our angel guides can we fully benefit from their empowering efforts.

The dream journal is an essential component of sleep strategies designed to explore our interactions with angels. Immediately upon awakening, daily entries are made in as much detail as possible, with particular attention given to recurring dreams, dream characters, and dream events. The dream journal enhances our recall and understanding of the dream experience, while specifically promoting our awareness of important angelic interactions.

Certain meditation approaches, along with self-hypnosis, can be used to discover angels and their empowering roles. "Angelic Power Discovery" is a three-pronged meditation strategy designed to access higher planes of power, to experience the presence of empowering angels, and to engage an empowering interaction with them. A quiet, softly lighted setting, and a comfortable, reclining position are recommended for the five-step procedure.

Angelic Power Discovery

Step 1   Let yourself become deeply relaxed by slowing your breathing and mentally scanning your body from your forehead down to your feet. Release the tension in your body until none remains. Let soothing relaxation soak into every muscle and joint. Let your mind become increasingly passive, as you banish all active thought. After a few moments of deep relaxation, imagine your total body enveloped by a rejuvenating glow of pure energy. Let yourself sense the pulsation of energy, particularly in your solar plexus region, as your total being is energized.

Step 2   As you remain relaxed, give yourself permission to engage higher planes of power, and to experience empowering interactions with angels. Imagine yourself entering an exquisitely manicured garden, with magnificent flowers which provide a festival of resplendent colors. Envision yourself following a path through the beautiful garden until you come to an inviting resting place. Settling back, perhaps on a comfortable bench or soft carpet of grass, you are tranquil and secure, at total peace with yourself, and at one with your surroundings.

Step 3   Envision gentle, radiant angels slowly gathering around you. Notice your sense of warm connectedness with them. You are comforted and empowered by their inspiring presence. As you interact with them, healthy energy fills your total being. One-by-one, they yield their empowering resources, and you graciously accept their generous gifts. Marvelous peace and healing flood your mind and body. Lingering in the garden, you are completely restored. You are at your peak of empowerment.

Step 4   Now leaving this wondrous place, you are mentally and physically infused with vitality. You are energized and attuned to the most powerful forces of the universe. You are radiating with energy and bathed in the light of health.

Step 5   As you reflect on the experience, affirm:

> *I am overflowing with power. Health and wellness are mine. The highest planes of power are available to me. I am surrounded by the presence of angels. I am protected and secure. I am empowered.*

You can return to the garden at will to engage its bountiful resources and to interact with its presence of angels.

With repeated practice of this procedure, you will probably find that the gathering of angels will vary; however, certain distinctive angels will usually come forth, and strongly empowering relationships will be established with them. Also, the presence of angels in your daily life will become increasingly evident, possibly because you become more attuned to their presence through your interactions with higher planes. The empowering benefits of Angelic Power Discovery, like many other health and fitness procedures, are accentuated by periodically reflecting on the experience, and reaffirming its empowering effects.

Among other promising procedures for accessing higher planes and communicating with angels is the use of tools and techniques such as the pendulum, automatic writing, and table tilting. When used as a gateway tool for tapping into higher dimensions, the recommended pendulum object is a quartz crystal suspended on a chain or string. When held over the hand, the object can provide answers to questions posed, by the direction of its motions. A to-and-fro motion typically signifies a "yes" response, whereas a side-to-side motion typically signifies a "no" response. A circular motion or the absence of movement typically signifies the non-availability of a "yes" or "no" answer. The pendulum can also be used with number and alphabet charts to provide detailed information beyond that available through other pendulum procedures.

Table-tilting is a group procedure in which a table, typically a card table, gives information through its tapping responses. For communicating with higher planes, a card table with legs of wood, rather than metal or other materials, is recommended. In this procedure, a group of four participants, with hands resting lightly on the top of the table, awaits spontaneous tilting, whereupon relevant questions are presented. The table typically responds through tapping movements, with one tap on the floor signifying "yes" and two taps signifying "no."

Automatic writing can be used open-endedly to spontaneously write complete messages, or it can be used as a sentence completion strategy. The pen is typically held in a writing position with the point resting lightly on the writing surface, as meaningful messages emerge in written communications.

The focus of psychic empowerment is on the undeveloped possibilities of our existence. When we look within ourselves, we are overwhelmed by the vastness of our undeveloped potential. When we look at the world, we are challenged by the endless opportunities surrounding us. When we look beyond our temporal reality, we are amazed at the awesome power and stunning beauty unfolding before us.

Through our interactions with angels, our consciousness is lifted to new levels, and our lives are enriched with exciting new possibilities. Mentally, physically, and spiritually, our total being is energized and empowered. Our existence takes on a new dimension of meaning and hope. Our empowering experiences with angels clearly affirm the unending splendor of our spiritual destiny.

✤ 10 ✤

A SEVEN-DAY HEALTH
AND FITNESS PLAN

The promise of an enriched, empowered life filled with health, happiness, and success belongs to everyone. In the previous pages, we have developed a psychic-empowerment model, which identifies the inner and outer sources of health and fitness readily available to all of us. We have examined the specialized skills which activate the dormant powers within ourselves. We have uncovered essential strategies and techniques formulated to tap into the limitless powers of the universe. While focusing on personal health and fitness goals, we have glimpsed the benefits of raised consciousness on a global scale.

The Seven-Day Health and Fitness Plan draws numerous concepts and procedures from the psychic-empowerment model, and organizes them into an approach which recognizes the essential physical, mental, and spiritual dimensions of health and fitness. This comprehensive plan is designed to facilitate an upward, endless growth spiral, in which our daily lives are enriched and empowered. Wherever we are in our personal growth and comfort zone, this plan, once implemented, shifts us forward with new purpose and power.

DAY ONE

Our psychic-empowerment plan begins on Day One by focusing on the basic, underlying factors which promote our mental and physical well-being. The specific objectives for Day One are first, to initiate a healthy, optimistic mental state at the beginning of the day, and second, to literally infuse the physical body with healthy energy, vitality, and rejuvenation. Two strategies are required to achieve these goals: The Awakening Empowerment Strategy and Star Gaze. These strategies lay the essential foundation for the remainder of the seven-day plan.

AWAKENING EMPOWERMENT STRATEGY

This strategy capitalizes on the awakening process by temporarily arresting it, and intervening with empowering imagery and affirmation. The procedure typically takes no more than a few minutes.

Step 1   *Momentary Passivity.* This step is a passive mental state, which allows resolution of the night's sleep experiences, including any interrupted stages or dream experiences. To facilitate transition, momentarily avoid all active thought.

Step 2   *Mind Scan.* The state of the mind is scanned as positive affirmations are formed. Positive mental elements are recognized and reinforced; all negative elements are identified and extinguished. Pessimism is replaced by optimism. Resignation is replaced by assertion. Hostility is replaced by goodwill. Remind yourself that good things come to people who expect them. Remind yourself that an unsinkable spirit is healthy and motivating.

Remind yourself that being filled with love and goodwill is healthy and rewarding both mentally and physically. Conclude the mental scan with the affirmation:

I am attuned within myself and with the world.

Step 3 *Body Scan.* Scan your physical body and mentally bathe it with positive energy. This process is facilitated by imagery of a healthy glow or radiance, enveloping and invigorating the body. Appropriate affirmations are then formed. Examples are:

I am at my physical best. I am infused with healthy energy and vigor.

Step 4 *Activities Scan.* Mentally scan your schedule for the day. Such a scan can highlight important activities, and suggest possible changes in plans. Crucial precognitive and clairvoyant impressions often emerge during this scan. It is important, at this phase, to be spontaneous and to give attention to the mind's intuitive process. Conclude the scan with the affirmation:

I am destined for success today.

The Awakening Empowerment Strategy is recommended for the remaining six days of the plan.

STAR GAZE

The second strategy for Day One, Star Gaze, was originally designed as a self-hypnotic-induction technique. It is often used, however, as a simple meditation procedure. This procedure is particularly effective in stimulating new growth factors, to form rejuvenating connections in the central nervous system. With repeated applications of Star Gaze, aging is effectively slowed, arrested, or even reversed, as vitality and new wellness energies are unleashed. Allow approximately thirty minutes, with no distractions, for the procedure.

Step 1   Assume a comfortable, reclining position and, with your eyes closed, envision a dark sky with a single star. Take plenty of time for the star to appear in bright, bold contrast to the dark sky. Once the star is visible, focus only on the star for a few moments, then envision four brilliant surrounding stars, all equally spaced around the central star. Continue focusing on the central star for several moments as you become increasingly relaxed.

Step 2   Beginning with one of the four surrounding stars, shift your focus clockwise from star to star, slowly counting the stars as you go: one, two, three, and four. Repeat this procedure, resting your gaze for a few moments on each of the four stars, while suggesting to yourself that you are becoming increasingly relaxed and responsive to your affirmations.

Step 3   Concentrate on the central star while expanding your peripheral vision to take in the four surrounding stars. Notice other stars of varying brilliance and color beginning to appear. Soon the sky is filled with a magnificent display of stars. Some appear alone and isolated, whereas others form glowing clusters or brilliant ribbons across the sky. Some gather to form intricate patterns and dazzling, geometric designs. Some appear nearby and pulsate with power; others are barely visible in the distant reaches of the universe.

Step 4 After scanning the star-studded heavens for a few moments, return to the star where you began. Note that it is now the brightest star in the sky. Continue gazing at the star as you affirm:

> *This is my personal star. It belongs to me. It is my contact with the universe. It symbolizes the unlimited potential within myself, and my capacity to reach beyond the borders of my present existence to experience the vastness of the universe. As I gaze at this star, I am becoming increasingly aware of the spark of divine power within myself. My innermost being is now pulsating with power. I am now empowered to achieve my loftiest goals, and to realize my highest potentials. The spark of light within myself is now a glowing, pulsating, rejuvenating force, infusing my body with youthful vigor and wellness.*

Step 5 Imagine the powerful, glowing light form at the solar plexus center of your body, reaching forth as a ray of light to connect you to your star in the heavens. Give your star a name—any name that comes to mind—and reaffirm that the powerful star belongs to you. As you remain connected to the star as a power source, draw energy from it and affirm:

> *The energies of youth and health are now permeating my body.*

Then imagine your body enveloped in a pulsating, rejuvenating glow, as you remain connected to your personal star. Focus on the inner core of glowing energy, and release your inner capacity for youth and wellness. Let sparkling, abounding energy flood your body with the glow of youth and wellness. Remind yourself that you are intimately connected to the illimitable power of the universe, and that your affirmations are promises of future realities.

Step 6   Focus on specific physical systems or organs, and energize them with healing, rejuvenating power. As you remain connected to your personal star, present the following affirmation:

> *Envisioning my personal star or calling its name at any time and under any circumstance will be instantly empowering to me.*

Step 7   End the procedure by suggesting:

> *As I count from one to five, I will become increasingly alert. On the count of five, I will be fully awake. One, two, three, four, and five.*

Following practice of this procedure, simply envisioning the star, or calling it by name, will instantly activate and magnify the empowering effects of this strategy.

DAY TWO

The goal of Day Two is to generate positive aura energies conducive to a healing and wellness interactions between the aura and the physical body. To achieve that important goal, two strategies are introduced. The Aura Health and Wellness Interaction, designed to energize either your own aura or that of another person, is used at a morning hour. The Aura Intervention Procedure, distributes positive energy throughout the body, and is intended to be used in the afternoon or evening. These procedures are highly effective in counteracting negative mental states such as fear, insecurity, and depression, all of which suppress the aura while exacting a heavy toll on the physical body. Each of these strategies requires approximately thirty minutes, in a comfortable setting free of distractions.

Aura Health and Wellness Interaction

Step 1 Settle back and mentally scan your body, pausing at points of stress and tension. Deliberately release the tension and infuse your total body with relaxation. Allow adequate time for your body to become fully relaxed, then affirm:

> *I am comfortable, relaxed, and secure.*

Step 2 Form images of a glowing blanket of bright energy at your feet, slowly rising to envelop your body. Allow adequate time for the blanket to enfold your total body, then affirm:

> *I am infused with positive, powerful energy. I am surrounded by the invigorating energies of good health and wellness.*

Step 3 Focus on the receiving target. If the target is yourself, form an image of your physical body, and allow the full body to soak in the glowing energies of health and wellness. Bathe your body systems and organs in the glow of health and vitality. If your target recipient is another person, form a mental image of that individual, then release radiant, healing energies as a glowing form which envelops the full body of the receiver. Stay with your recipient for a few moments, as the energies of health and wellness are being absorbed.

Step 4   Conclude by affirming:

> *I am now infused with positive aura energy and potential. I am empowered to use these resources to enrich my life and the lives of others.*

The second strategy for Day Two is the Aura Intervention Procedure, designed to liberate submerged aura energies, replenish the external aura, and generate a healthy, positive interaction between the aura system and the physical body.

AURA INTERVENTION PROCEDURE

Step 1   Settle back and let yourself become comfortable and relaxed. With your eyes closed, form an image of a powerful, internal, super energy core in the central region of your body. Picture the core as a glowing inner vertical bar of powerful energy.

Step 2   Mentally release powerful energy from the central energy core to radiate throughout your physical body. Flood your total body with positive, vitalizing, rejuvenating energy.

Step 3   Focus on particular organs and systems, bathing them in the glow of powerful energy. Allow plenty of time for your body to absorb this invigorating energy.

Step 4   Permit the energy emitted from the central energy core to extend beyond your body as a brilliant, radiating energy force.

Step 5 Conclude by affirming:

> *I am infused with abundant energy. I am enveloped in a radiant glow of health and vitality. My total being in revitalized and invigorated with positive energy. I am empowered.*

The effectiveness of these intervention procedures is strengthened through an empowering gesture known as finger interlock. Requiring only seconds to implement, the technique is executed by simply joining the thumb and middle finger of each hand, then bringing them together to form interlocking circles, while mentally enveloping the body in a shield of positive energy. Finger interlock is also useful as an instant relaxation technique. It can be applied as often as desired for the remainder of the plan and thereafter.

DAY THREE

Among our major sources of health and physical fitness are the higher, intangible planes of power. The goal of Day Three is to engage out-of-body travel, in order to access these higher sources of health and fitness. Astral Trek and OBEs Interdimensional Interaction are the preferred strategies for achieving that goal. Like other OBE-induction procedures, these strategies require conditions similar to those conducive to sleep. A comfortable, reclining position with legs uncrossed and hands resting at the sides is recommended. Lighting should be subdued. Each procedure requires thirty to forty minutes, during which there are absolutely no distractions. A period of at least two hours should separate the applications of these procedures.

Astral Trek

Step 1   With your eyes closed, slow your breathing and relax your body. For this procedure, relaxation begins at the feet and culminates at the forehead. Mentally scan your body from your feet upward, forming a mental picture of your physical body at rest. Arrest your scan at stress points, and replace any build-up of tension with soothing relaxation. Upon reaching your forehead, mentally bathe your body in glowing energy, as you affirm:

> *I am safe, comfortable, and relaxed. As I prepare to leave my body, I am protected and secure. As I travel from my body, I will remain enveloped in a powerful shield of protection. Nothing can harm me as I travel out-of-body to experience other realities. I am empowered to return to my body with comfort and ease at any moment I decide to do so.*

Step 2   As relaxation deepens, form a mental picture of your body at rest. Notice the position of your body and the details of your clothing. Envision yourself suspended above your body, looking down from above. Allow yourself to drift away from your body while remaining connected to it by a brilliant cord of glowing energy.

Step 3   Envision a peaceful scene, such as a familiar river, mountain range, or skyline at sunset. Absorb the peaceful tranquillity of the scene, then introduce motion into your imagery such as billowy clouds, floating balloons, ripples in water, or possibly, a slowly drifting boat.

Step 4   Envision yourself engaging a higher plane of radiant light. As you interact with that plane, allow the silver cord to become a channel for transporting healthy energy to your body at rest. While remaining suspended in space, affirm:

> *I am now out of my body. I am empowered and in full command of my faculties. I am attuned to the unlimited powers of the universe. I can now draw from the universe abundant power to energize my total being.*

As you continue to envision the silver cord as a powerful channel connecting you to your physical body, mentally infuse your body with healthy energy. Bathe specific organs, and energize particular bodily functions.

Step 5 To return to your physical body and end the OBE state, view your body from a distance and affirm:

> *I am now ready to return to my body.*

Gently allow yourself to descend as a light form, merging with your physical body. Focus your attention on your breathing and other physical sensations. Before opening your eyes, affirm:

> *I am now at one with my total being—physically, mentally, and spiritually. I am fully empowered in mind, body, and spirit.*

Step 6 The procedure is concluded by a brief period of reflection and reaffirmation of the empowering benefits of the experience.

OBEs Interdimensional Interaction

Step 1 Apply Steps One through Four of Astral Trek to induce the desired out-of-body state.

Step 2 *Astral Memory.* While you remain in the out-of-body state, select a significant early memory from your childhood and focus on the experience. Notice the peaceful tranquillity the memory evokes. Allow the experience and its physical setting to become increasingly vivid in your mind.

Step 3 *Astral Travel.* Give yourself permission to travel to the site of the early experience. Use imagery of the target destination to guide your astral journey. Upon reaching your destination, which usually requires only a few minutes, view the physical setting from above. Note any changes in the setting that may have occurred since the early experience. Envision the early experience once again, and let yourself absorb the full pleasure of the memory.

Step 4 *Astral Light.* As the memory fades, let yourself become increasingly aware of a brilliant dimension of light in the distance. Bathed in its glow, let yourself be drawn toward the light source.

Step 5 *Power Infusion.* Upon approaching the edge of the light source, but without entering it, permit its emission of pure energy to permeate your total being. Allow yourself to engage radiant beams of light which fill and overflow your being with power.

Step 6 *Power Transfer.* Envision your physical body at rest in the distance and transfer overflowing power to it.

Allow a stream of pure light to flow through the silver cord and infuse your physical body with powerful energy. Fill your body to capacity with wellness and vitality. Bathe every part of your body in healing energy. Target particular areas of dysfunction or weakness and empower them with healthy vigor.

Step 7 *Astral Return.* Without terminating the infusion process, give yourself permission to return to your physical body resting peacefully in the distance. Focusing your attention on your body and its surroundings is usually sufficient to initiate the astral return.

Step 8. *Astral Re-entry.* End the astral experience, and re-enter your physical body by focusing on breathing and other physical sensations. Before opening your eyes, affirm:

I am fully empowered.

In Step Four of this procedure, which introduces a higher dimension of light, you may experience a gentle, magnanimous presence in the form of a spiritual guide or angel. In repeated trials, the presence typically remains unchanged. Though not designed specifically for that purpose, this procedure can be applied to identify and come to know your spiritual guides or guardian angels.

DAY FOUR

Day Four of our plan introduces two major strategies for developing PK potentials for health and fitness. The PK Prescription Procedure focuses on the positive mental and physical conditions known to be conducive to empowering PK; the PK Formula for Health and Fitness generates a peak empowerment state, and disperses healthy energy to specific physical organs and systems. The PK Prescription can be followed immediately by the PK Formula. Each procedure requires a quiet setting for a period of approximately thirty minutes.

PK Prescription Procedure

This strategy is designed to activate healthy PK and release the flow of healthy energy throughout the body. Disabling thoughts are uprooted, the mental and physical expressions of failure are intercepted, and disempowering attitudes and emotions are disarmed.

Step 1 *Affirmation.* As you settle back and relax, affirm your goal of becoming more fully empowered, with the capacity to use your PK potentials for good health:

> *My goal is to become an empowered person. I am prepared to take command of my life and bring forth positive change. I am becoming balanced with my true self. I am discovering the essence of my inner being. My PK faculties are now available to me. I will find ways of tapping into my psychic powers and releasing them to enrich my life with health and wellness.*

> *I am capable of changing my life. By looking inward, I will discover my true, inner self and its positive potentials. I will replace the toxic waste of negative attitudes and emotions with positive, empowering resources. I will reverse negative thoughts with positive affirmations. I will unleash new growth potential in my life.*

Step 2 *Focusing.* The objective of Step Two is to focus introspectively on existing attitudes, beliefs, and emotions, in an effort to identify, examine, and replace disempowering elements with empowering ones. Areas of focus include, but are not limited to:

- *The Inner Self.* Identify specific disempowering concepts and expectations. Remind yourself that you are a person of dignity and incomparable worth. Remind yourself that you have an unlimited supply of inner resources. Tell yourself emphatically, *I love who I am.* Uproot expectations of failure and toss them out.

- *Beliefs.* Identify disempowering beliefs. Banish and replace them with positive convictions. Remind yourself that you do not have to be all things to all people. Being true to yourself is more important than pleasing others. View your imperfections as challenges, not irreversible faults. Think of your problems as opportunities, not barriers. Think of your failures and misfortunes as temporary setbacks, not horrible disasters. Remind yourself that success, like life, is a process, not a product. Tell yourself that you are a work in progress. Remind yourself that as you grow and develop, you are succeeding. Recognize your weaknesses, but do not use them as excuses—use your strengths to compensate for your weaknesses. Remind yourself that you are a self-made person. The world, the culture, and your environment provide the raw material, but you build your own life. You are what you choose to be.

- *Emotions.* Remind yourself that your feelings are important and worth listening to. Get them out and address them. Become aware of them as valid expressions of your innermost self. Pay attention to your negative as well as positive feelings. Use positive self-talk to build feelings of worth and expectations of success. Expressing yourself is healthy and empowering, both mentally and physically.

- *Attitude.* The empowerment attitude asserts, *I am filled with unlimited potential, and surrounded by unlimited opportunities.* The empowerment attitude is a "take-charge" state of mind. It is solution-oriented, rather than problem-centered. It emphasizes positive possibilities, rather than negative probabilities. It looks at the total situation, not the down side only. It copes actively with adversity, rather than passively yielding to it. It views even personal suffering as potentially empowering. It finds opportunities for choice and room for action, even in the most restrictive situation. The empowerment attitude can be summed up with the positive affirmation, *I am empowered.* With frequent use, that affirmation becomes more and more empowering.

On the surface, focusing on the self, beliefs, emotions, and attitudes may seem unrelated to PK. Remember,

however, that by generating positive conditions conducive to PK, you unlock inner sources of health, and
prepare the PK faculty to distribute powerful healing
and wellness energy throughout your body.

Step 3 *Infusion.* The focusing step now complete, assume a
reflective state of mind, and allow the empowerment
products of focusing to be absorbed into the innermost
part of your self. Envision the central core of your
being as a powerful, glowing magnet, attracting positive energy, while repelling anything negative. Allow a
few moments for this infusion process to complete
itself. As the reflective state continues, allow your PK
powers to become activated to disperse health and
vitality throughout your body. Allow physical organs
and functions to be spontaneously targeted and
infused with healthy energy.

PK FORMULA FOR HEALTH AND FITNESS

This four-step procedure activates PK and focuses it on
specific health and fitness targets.

Step 1 *Sensate Focusing.* Center your full attention on your
physical body and its sensations. With your eyes
closed, notice areas of coolness, warmth, tension, tingling, numbness, and pressure. Zero in on specific sensations, study them, and practice altring them. For
example, replace coolness with warmth and tension
with relaxation. Substitute numbness for tingling, and
move pressure points to other locations. Allow the various sensations to become smooth and pleasurable.

Step 2 *Energizing PK Systems.* As your eyes remain closed, energize your physical and mental systems by mentally scanning your body from your head downward, as you envision a soft blanket of energy accompanying the scan and enveloping your body. Breathe deeply as you envision a powerful core of pulsating energy in your solar plexus region. Allow the vibrant energy generated by the central core to permeate your total body.

Step 3 *Balancing PK Systems.* To balance your PK energy systems, bring the tips of your fingers together in a praying-hands position. Hold the position for a few moments as you affirm:

> *I am energized and balanced with PK power.*

Sense the balancing exchange of powerful energy at your fingertips. You are now at your energized peak.

Step 4 *PK Energy Release.* Center your full attention on the PK target—internal organs, biological systems, or fitness goals. As you focus on the target, envision the desired PK outcomes. Allow a powerful beam of PK energy to permeate the target. Permit the energy release to intensify in brilliance as needed to achieve the desired results. Close down the energy release by again focusing on the central energy core of your solar plexus region. Affirm:

> *I am empowered with the energies of health and physical fitness.*

The PK Formula can be adapted to any health and fitness need. While not essential, relevant knowledge of physiology facilitates application of this procedure.

DAY FIVE

Day Five of our plan presents two major health and fitness strategies. The Psychic Protection Procedure introduces techniques to energize and protect the self, while Numbers uses numerological concepts and empowering affirmations to induce an empowered sleep state.

PSYCHIC PROTECTION PROCEDURE

> The Psychic Protection Procedure is used in personal empowerment to neutralize and release any disempowering forces surrounding the self, while protecting the self from any residual effects or further invasion of negative energy. The procedure replenishes our positive energy supply and prevents further depletion of our energy system.

Step 1   Envision a higher dimension of pure, white light and a channel of energy connecting you to it. Imagine positive energy streaming into your being and enveloping your body with a sparkling, radiant shield of power. Affirm:

> *I am fully enveloped and infused with positive energy. I am empowered to repel the onslaught of negative forces. I am fully empowered in mind and body.*

Step 2   Bring the fingers of both hands together in a praying hands position to balance your energy system. Affirm:

> *The systems of my being are in perfect harmony. I am saturated mentally and physically with positive energy.*

Step 3   Conclude the procedure by joining the thumbs and middle fingers to form interlocking circles, a technique which prevents depletion of your energy supply. Affirm:

> *I am at my peak of mental and physical empow-erment. I am protected and secure.*

NUMBERS PROCEDURE

This procedure is implemented just prior to sleep. It is based on numerology, which holds that each number has a vibratory energy and significance beyond its simple expression of quantity. The procedure involves counting backwards from nine to one, as each number is visualized in some impressive way. You may, for instance, see the numbers being formed by white clouds against a peaceful blue sky, or your may imagine them being exquisitely painted by an artist on canvas. You may project the numbers boldly on the full moon, or envision them being formed by stars in the night sky.

Each number, once it is clearly visualized, is accompanied by appropriate empowering affirmations. The affirmations, which are consistent with the number's numerological significance, can be revised to meet specific personal needs. In this procedure, the combination of number images and related affirmations are doubly empowering.

Begin Numbers by lying down and, just before going to sleep, focusing on your breathing. Clear your mind of active thought, then, with your eyes closed, affirm:

> *I am now prepared to enter peaceful, restful sleep. As I sleep, I will be protected and secure.*

Upon awakening, I will feel revitalized and refreshed. The powers of the numbers I envision and the affirmations I present to myself will be absorbed deeply into my subconscious mind to empower me in mind, body, and spirit.

Following this general affirmation, form a clear image of each number, one at a time. As vivid imagery of a particular number unfolds, present the affirmations relevant to that number as follows:

Number 9.

This number signals my oneness with the universe. All the powers of the universe are at my command. I can tap into them at any moment to energize my life with health, happiness, and fulfillment. I am now attuned to the unlimited powers of the universe. Whenever I envision the number nine, I will be instantly empowered with the positive energies of the universe.

Number 8.

This number vibrates with success and fulfillment. Mentally, physically, and spiritually, I am attuned to these vibrations. I am filled with potential and surrounded by success. The energies of this number are an integral part of my being. When I envision the number eight, I am reminded that success is my destiny.

Number 7.

> *The number seven is the promise of continued growth and knowledge. Knowledge is power. By probing the inexhaustible mysteries of the universe, I am empowered with increased awareness and new understanding of my own life. The light of unlimited insight and enriched existence surrounds this number. By envisioning the number seven, I am filled with the positive energies of wholeness—a sound mind, healthy body, and soaring spirit.*

Number 6.

> *The constancy of my identity and the totality of my being are represented by this number. I am, at this moment in time, a product of my past, as well as a work in progress. From the beginning, my life has been a continuous progression of growth and an accumulation of experience. Each moment, my endless journey continues, as the unlimited opportunities of the future constantly unfold.*

Number 5.

> *The adventures of life and the excitement of daily living are represented by the number five. Each moment of my life is filled with gladness, opportunity, and thrilling possibility. Each passing day, I discover something new about myself and the totality of my existence. I relish my existence in the here and now.*

Number 4.

The vibrations of this number are firm and unwavering. They reveal the power of my inner faith and steadfast trust in myself. This number represents the constancy of my present existence and my hope for the future. I am empowered to move in unison with the universe to achieve my highest destiny. The ominous forces which threaten my existence are vulnerable to the powers of faith and trust which infuse my life with vitality, purpose, and well-being.

Number 3.

This number is a reminder of my unique talents and powers of adaptation. I value the richness of my life. My inner resources equip me to improve the quality of my life while contributing to the needs around me. I value change and new opportunities for growth and self-discovery. Even when constricted by circumstances, I discover new options and opportunities. I am empowered to cope with adversity and benefit from it. My powers of adaptation extend to my physical body to promote wellness and healthy biological functions. When I envision the number three, I will be instantly infused with vigor and healthy energy.

Number 2.

Antithesis and balance emanate from this number. Mentally and physically, I am balanced, energized, and empowered. My mind and body are exquisitely attuned to the energies of the universe. My mind is in harmony with my total being. The systems of my body are at equilibrium. I am enveloped with the glow of health and wellness. By envisioning the number two, I will immediately infuse my life with balance, health, and wellness.

Number 1.

This number signifies purpose and action. My life is filled with meaning and bountiful energy. I am empowered to act and achieve. Nothing can stop me once I make up my mind. I will use my potentials to enrich my life and the lives of others. Whenever I envision the number one, I will be instantly empowered with purpose and vitality.

At this point, having completed the backwards counting and related affirmations, you will probably be very drowsy and deeply relaxed. If you find yourself falling asleep before you finish the procedure, you can simply scan the remain numbers as you affirm:

The power of these numbers are now being absorbed deeply into my being.

End the procedure with the following affirmation:

As I now drift into restful sleep, the power of these numbers will permeate my total being. I will remain empowered mentally, physically, and spiritually. I will awaken refreshed and revitalized.

If you remain awake following this procedure, you can facilitate sleep by imagining that you are suspended in air, perhaps on a soft, fluffy cloud drifting gently in the breeze.

With practice, simply visualizing a given number within the context of its positive numerological significance will activate the number's frequency, and lead to an infusion of powerful energy.

DAY SIX

The goals for Day Six are to activate the health and fitness potential of the pyramid as an empowerment tool, and to open a gateway to the power within yourself and the limitless power of the universe. Two major procedures, Ascending the Pyramid II and Crown of Power, will help to achieve these goals.

ASCENDING THE PYRAMID II

> This procedure is built around imagery of a pyramid with ten steps, each inscribed with a word which gives rise to related empowering affirmations. Essentially a meditation procedure, Ascending the Pyramid II is initiated by closing the eyes, progressively relaxing the body, and envisioning a pyramid with ten steps leading to its apex. Each step, with its inscription, is then envisioned in sequence, beginning at the first step and culminating at the apex, as empowering affirmations are presented.

Step 1   Insight.

> *Insight is power. Insight and self-understanding increase my potential for a healthy, fulfilled, and*

empowered life. I will use my powers of insight to enrich my life mentally, physically, and spiritually.

Step 2   Enrichment.

My life is an exciting journey of growth and discovery. I possess within myself a rich and bountiful supply of healthy energy. I am empowered to unleash my inner resources and distribute them as needed. I am empowered to tap into the higher planes of the universe to enrich my life with boundless health and vigor.

Step 3   Focus.

I am focused inwardly and outwardly in my quest for a rich, empowered life. My inner powers constantly interact to keep me centered and balanced. Mentally, physically, and spiritually, my total being is at equilibrium.

Step 4   Vitality.

I am empowered with health and vigor. My body is constantly revitalizing and renewing itself. My immune and defense systems are fortified and empowered to keep me healthy and physically fit.

Step 5   Rejuvenation.

My potential for rejuvenation is strong and enduring. Youthful energy is flowing throughout my total being. The vital organs and systems of my body are constantly energized and rejuvenated.

Step 6   Wellness.

> *Each day, I am becoming healthier and more full of energy. Wellness energies are being constantly unleashed to fortify every cell and fiber of my body. Empowered with abundant wellness energy, I am at my best mentally and physically.*

Step 7   Oneness.

> *I am an elegantly designed creation, made of many parts constantly working together as one. My body, mind, and spirit are a smoothly functioning unit, perfectly organized in an intricate framework. I am at oneness and peace with myself and the universe.*

Step 8   Intervention.

> *I am empowered to intervene as needed to promote my mental and physical well-being. I am empowered to banish threats to my health and replace them with the positive energies of wellness. All my inner resources and the unlimited powers of the universe are at my command.*

Step 9   Attunement.

> *The complex parts of my being are a symphony of beauty and perfection. I am an efficient, harmonious energy system. I am attuned to the inner universe of my being and to the outer universe of unlimited power.*

Step 10 Empowerment.

> *In my capacity to be more aware of my body and its needs, to enrich my life with healthy energy, to maintain mental and physical stability, to become infused with vitality, to activate and distribute rejuvenating energies, to promote wellness, to experience oneness and peace with myself and the universe, to intervene into my physical system as needed, and to achieve a state of healthy attunement, both inwardly and outwardly, I am fully empowered with abundant health and physical fitness.*

As your eyes remain closed, envision yourself pausing at the pyramid's apex, your hands, like powerful antennae, reaching upward toward the higher planes of the universe. Allow your body to become even more empowered with positive energy. Ascending the Pyramid II is concluded with the simple affirmation:

> *I am empowered.*

CROWN OF POWER PROCEDURE

This procedure incorporates imagery of a bejeweled crown, in a strategy designed as a gateway to the hidden powers within yourself and the outer universe. Although formulated specifically for health and rejuvenation purposes, the procedure can be adapted to any personal empowerment goal.

To begin the procedure, settle back and fully relax your body. Then, with your eyes closed, imagine your inner being as a vast, magnificent kingdom, surrounded by a great wall with immense gates. Envision yourself approaching the massive gates, and opening them by a simple touch of the hand. As you step inside the gates, envision yourself instantly enveloped in a glow of radiant energy. Take a few moments to absorb the peace and serenity of your surroundings.

Now, picture before you an exquisite palace of marble, glistening in the light. Its doors are magnificently carved, and its roof is a towering crystal dome. Upon approaching the palace, you stand in amazement at its resplendent beauty. A touch of your hand is sufficient to open its doors upon even greater splendor. As you step inside, you are enveloped and energized with radiant light streaming from the dazzling crystal dome.

Envision in the center of the expansive room a marble pedestal, upon which rests a magnificent, bejeweled crown, bathed in light from the crystal dome. You are inexorably drawn to the crown, aware that it is your link to the power within yourself and the limitless power of the universe.

Envision yourself standing before the pedestal, then reaching forth to touch the crown. It is the touch which penetrates the infinite power of the universe. The instant outpouring of healthy, rejuvenating energy is all-consuming. The overflow of power permeates your total being.

Envision yourself calmly lifting the exquisite crown and placing it upon your head. The infusion of powerful energy is again immediate and intense. You can, at this moment, have your heart's desire—wisdom, health, happiness, wealth, success—all of these and more. Whatever you affirm at this moment is your destiny. Power, peace of mind, rejuvenation, and abundant wellness—they are now yours. Endless possibilities surround you. Unlimited potential exists within you, awaiting your command to empower and enrich your life. You are the master of your destiny. Your total being—mind, body, and spirit—is fully energized and empowered.

As you remove the crown and return it to its place on the pedestal, the infusion of power continues uninterrupted. Upon now leaving the palace, you remind yourself that you can return to it at will to explore the vastness of its empowering resources. With the kingdom now behind you, you are aware that it belongs to you; it is your inner universe of unlimited power.

The Crown of Power Touch can be used to reactivate the empowering effects of this procedure. Lift your hands and touch the area of your forehead which supported the envisioned crown—a symbolic gesture of the bountiful power within your reach at any moment. This non-intrusive gesture requires only seconds and can be used almost anywhere.

DAY SEVEN

The goals for this final day of our health and fitness plan are to tap into the highest powers of the universe through our interactions with nature, to engage empowering interactions with angels, and to contribute to the empowerment needs of the planet. Three procedures—Tree Power Interfusion, Angelic Power Discovery, and Global Intervention Procedure—are used to achieve these goals.

Tree Power Interfusion provides a direct, physical link to the concentrated healing and wellness energies of nature, as manifested in the majestic tree. In many ways, the energy systems of the tree parallel the complex systems of our own physiology. The tree provides the ideal channel for an empowering interaction with nature.

TREE POWER INTERFUSION

Step 1 Select a tree, preferably a large one, that appeals to you and seems appropriate for your empowerment goals. Pay particular attention to the stateliness of the tree—its height, shape, and colors.

Step 2 Rest your hands on the tree and note its unique features. Notice the patterns and texture of its bark. Stroke the tree and sense its power. Notice the responsiveness of the tree as your energies merge with it.

Step 3 Envision the tree as a giant antenna piercing the unlimited power sources of the universe. As your hands continue to rest on the tree, envision the inner core of your own energy system radiating powerful energy. Allow the energies of your being to interact with the energies of the tree. Notice the physical vibration of that interaction and the infusion of positive energy. Allow the physical infusion to continue, until you are overflowing with powerful energy.

Step 4 Conclude the infusion process by again stroking the tree, as you mentally express gratitude and recognition of its splendor and power.

The empowering effects of this procedure can be amplified by leaning against the tree, with your back resting against the tree trunk, and affirming:

The energies of my being are balanced and attuned to the powers of this tree and the universe. I am infused with health and vitality. I am fortified with positive growth potential. Mentally, physically, and spiritually, I am empowered.

ANGELIC POWER DISCOVERY

Angelic Power Discovery is specifically designed to reveal the presence of angels in our lives and initiate an empowering interaction with them. A quiet, softly lighted setting and a comfortable, reclining position are recommended for the five-step procedure.

Step 1 Let yourself become deeply relaxed by slowing your breathing and mentally scanning your body from your forehead to your feet. Release the tension in your body until none remains. Let soothing relaxation soak into every muscle and joint. Let your mind become increasingly passive, as you banish all active thought. After a few moments of deep relaxation, imagine your total body enveloped by a rejuvenating glow of pure energy. Let yourself sense the pulsation of energy, particularly in your solar plexus region, as your total being is energized.

Step 2 As you remain relaxed, give yourself permission to engage higher planes of power and to experience empowering interactions with angels. Imagine yourself entering an exquisitely manicured garden, with magnificent flowers providing a festival of resplendent colors. Envision yourself following a winding path through the beautiful garden until you come to an inviting resting place. Settling back, perhaps on a comfortable bench or the soft carpet of grass, you are tranquil and secure, at total peace with yourself, and at oneness with your surroundings.

Step 3   Envision gentle, radiant angels slowly gathering around you. Notice your sense of warm connectedness with them. You are comforted and empowered by their inspiring presence. As you interact with them, healthy energy fills your total being. One-by-one, they yield their empowering resources; and you graciously accept their generous gifts. Marvelous peace and healing flood your mind and body. Lingering in the garden, you are completely restored. You are at your peak of empowerment.

Step 4   Now leaving this wondrous place, you are mentally and physically infused with vitality. You are energized and attuned to the most powerful forces of the universe. You are radiating with energy and bathed in the light of health.

Step 5   As you reflect on the experience, affirm:

> I am overflowing with power. Health and wellness
> are mine. The highest planes of power are available
> to me. I am surrounded by the presence of angels. I
> am protected and secure. I am empowered.

You can return to the garden at will to engage its bountiful resources and to interact with its presence of angels.

The empowering benefits of Angelic Power Discovery, like many other health and fitness procedures, are accentuated by periodically reflecting on the experience and reaffirming its empowering effects.

Global Intervention Procedure

We conclude our seven-day health and fitness plan by turning our attention to the planet and its needs. The Global Intervention Procedure is a strategy designed first, to bathe the planet in revitalizing energy, and second, to meet particular earth needs. Although the procedure was originally designed for groups, it is adapted here for individual use. In global empowerment, our individual efforts unite with a larger energy force, already set in motion by the empowerment contributions of other individuals.

Step 1   A globe, if available, is situated to permit easy viewing. In the absence of a globe, imagery of the earth can be equally effective.

Step 2   Reflect on general and specific earth needs, then formulate your global objectives. A few examples are global peace, an end to human and animal suffering, strengthening the globe's ozone layer, revitalizing forests, and empowering an endangered species.

Step 3   Personalize the planet and address it as follows:

> As the living planet, you are a part of me and I am a part of you. Your well-being facilitates my well-being. The healthy conditions which empower you also empower me. The toxic forces which weaken you likewise weaken me.
>
> You give support and power to me daily. I now give support and power to you. I enfold you with positive energy and encircle you with the light of peace.

Step 4 Follow these affirmations of caring and commitment with a few moments of silence, in which you envision the planet surrounded with the glow of invigorating energy. Actively infuse the earth with this energy. Accompany your empowering imagery and affirmations with sending gestures, such as turning the palms of your hands toward the globe to facilitate the infusion effort.

Step 5 Focus on specific empowerment objectives. Present appropriate affirmations as you envision desired effects in as much detail as possible. For example, revitalizing a devastated forest could include envisioning the near-dead forest and addressing it with the affirmation:

> *You are now revitalized with powerful growth energy.*

Followed this with empowering imagery of the forest coming alive with towering trees, prolific foliage, lush undergrowth, and teeming animal life. You can further personalize your empowerment efforts by envisioning yourself as part of the energized forest, interacting with its wondrous mix of excitement and tranquillity.

Step 6 Conclude the procedure by reaffirming your commitment to empower the earth.

Psychic empowerment applied on a global scale is important because of its capacity to initiate a global rebuilding process. By actively intervening into global problems, we can reverse the onslaught of destructive forces disempowering the earth. We can discover effective ways to create global change, and make the earth a safer and healthier place for ourselves and the generations to follow.

CONCLUSION

Our Seven-Day Health and Fitness Plan now complete, we have taken a giant step toward a more fully empowered life. The plan is the beginning, not the end, of an exciting journey of endless growth and fulfillment. Equipped with psychic knowledge and a vision of the future, we are empowered with unlimited potential and boundless opportunity. Perhaps most importantly, we are empowered moment by moment with the matchless beauty of our existence and the wondrous destiny awaiting each of us.

GLOSSARY

Angelic Power Discovery. A procedure designed to uncover the presence of angels and engage them in an empowering interaction.

Ascending the Pyramid II. A meditative strategy that uses imagery of the pyramid and related affirmations to promote health and physical fitness.

Astral Trek. An out-of-body, self-induction procedure designed specifically to infuse the body with healthful energy.

aura. A field of energy surrounding the body and believed by some to represent the inner life force.

Aura Caress. A procedure that evaluates the frequency patterns of the human aura.

Aura Hand Viewing Technique. An aura viewing procedure in which the aura patterns around the hand become visible.

Aura Health and Wellness Interaction Procedure. A procedure that generates positive aura energies, and initiates a healing and wellness interaction between the aura and the physical body.

Aura Intervention Procedure. A procedure designed to liberate submerged aura energies, replenish the external aura, and generate a positive interaction between the aura and the physical body.

Aura Massage. A technique that balances the aura and releases blocked energies.

autohypnosis. See self-hypnosis.

Awakening Empowerment Strategy. A procedure which temporarily arrests awakening from the sleep process and presents empowering affirmations.

clairvoyance. The psychic perception of objects, conditions, situations, or events.

Cognitive Relaxation Trance Procedure. A hypnotic induction procedure in which the body is progressively relaxed as suggestions of responsiveness are presented.

Cosmic Transcendence Strategy. A procedure that uses imagery and affirmation prior to sleep to activate increased awareness of higher realities during the deepest stages of sleep.

Crown of Power. A procedure that incorporates imagery of a crown as a gateway tool to the inner and outer universe.

Crystal Interactive Programming. A step-by-step procedure designed to program an empowering interaction with the quartz crystal.

Dream Intervention Strategy. A procedure designed to initiate empowering dreams, or to intervene into the dream experience.

Energy Transfer Strategy. A procedure designed to add healthful energy to the aura system.

Environmental Clearing and Reprogramming. A procedure that intervenes into negative environmental situations, and dismantles and re-programs disempowering conditions.

ESP. See extrasensory perception.

extrasensory perception (ESP). The knowledge of, or response to, events, conditions, and situations independently of known sensory mechanisms or processes.

Finger Interlock. A relaxation procedure that prevents depletion of the aura system.

Finger Spread Technique. A trance induction and sleep arrest procedure in which the fingers are spread in a tense position as suggestions or affirmations are presented.

Fitness Through Gazing. A crystal gazing procedure that focuses on specific health and fitness goals.

Focal Point Technique. An aura viewing technique in which the eyes focus on a small, shiny object, such as a silver star, situated on a background screen.

Focal Shift Technique. An aura viewing technique in which the eyes are permitted to shift out of focus.

Gateway Intervention Procedure. A procedure designed to access and activate health and wellness during sleep.

Global Intervention Procedure. A strategy designed to bathe the planet with energy and meet particular earth needs.

Hand Levitation Technique. A hypnotic induction procedure in which the hand rises gently toward the forehead to induce the trance state.

hypnagogic sleep. A hypnotic-like, drowsy state preceding sleep.

hypnopompic sleep. The semiconscious state preceding waking.

hypnoproduction. The emergence of new potentials and full-blown skills in the hypnotic state.

hypnosis. An altered state of consciousness in which susceptibility to suggestion is heightened.

Immune Empowerment Formula. An out-of-body strategy designed to empower the immune system.

Induction by Intent. An advanced hypnotic self-induction procedure that induces a trance state by sheer intent alone.

ironic effect. An effect opposite of that expected.

Master of Pain. An out-of-body procedure designed to manage pain and promote wellness.

Moment of Power. A strategy designed to promote interaction with a model of the pyramid in an effort to increase inner power.

Mutual Crystal Gazing. A crystal gazing strategy designed to initiate a positive energy exchange between two participants.

NDE. See near-death experience.

near-death experience (NDE). An experience in which death appears imminent, often accompanied by a sense of separation of consciousness from the biological body.

Numbers. A procedure based on numerology for promoting empowering sleep.

Numerology. The study of numbers and their significance beyond the expression of quantity.

OBE. See out-of-body experience.

OBEs Interdimensional Interaction. An out-of-body procedure designed to initiate an empowering interaction with higher dimensions of positive energy.

out-of-body experience (OBE). A state of awareness in which the locus of perception shifts, resulting in a conscious sense of being in a spatial location away from the physical body.

out-of-body PK. The capacity to influence matter or motion while in the out-of-body state. See psychokinesis.

Pain Confrontation Approach. An assertive pain management procedure which establishes control over pain and banishes it.

Peripheral Glow Technique. A hypnotic induction procedure involving the expansion of peripheral vision.

PK. See psychokinesis.

PK Formula for Health and Fitness. A procedure designed to activate PK and focus it on health and fitness.

PK Prescription Procedure. A procedure designed to activate inner PK mechanisms and release the flow of healthful energy.

precognition. The psychic awareness of the future.

Psychic Protection Procedure. A procedure formulated to release disempowering influences around the self while protecting the self from residual effect or further invasion of negative forces.

Pre-sleep Intervention Procedure. A procedure designed to intervene into the out-of-body process as it occurs just prior to sleep.

psychic vampirism. The tendency of some aura systems to drain other systems of energy.

psychokinesis (PK). The capacity of the mind to influence objects, events, and processes in the apparent absence of intervening physical energy or intermediary instrumentation.

replacement imagery. The use of imagery of an object, such as a crystal or pyramid, in the object's physical absence to achieve personal empowerment goals.

self-hypnosis. A self-induced altered state of consciousness in which the induction, deepening, and management procedures are implemented and controlled by the subject independently of a hypnotist. Also called autohypnosis.

Star Gaze. A meditative-like procedure which uses imagery of stars to induce a hypnotic trance.

telepathy. The psychic sending and receiving of cognitive and affective contents.

Therapeutic Exchange Procedure. A pain management procedure designed to replace pain with soothing relaxation.

Tree Power Interfusion. A procedure formulated to engage the tree as a natural source of energy in an empowering interaction.

Upward Gaze. A hypnotic induction procedure in which the subject gazes upward while slowly closing the eyes.

INDEX

STAY IN TOUCH

On the following pages you will find listed, with their current prices, some of the books now available on related subjects. Your book dealer stocks most of these and will stock new titles in the Llewellyn series as they become available. We urge your patronage.

TO GET A FREE CATALOG

You are invited to write for our bimonthly news magazine/catalog, Llewellyn's *New Worlds of Mind and Spirit*. A sample copy is free, and it will continue coming to you at no cost as long as you are an active mail customer. Or you may subscribe for just $10 in the United States and Canada ($20 overseas, first class mail). Many bookstores also have New Worlds available to their customers. Ask for it.

In *New Worlds* you will find news and features about new books, tapes and services; announcements of meetings and seminars; helpful articles; author interviews and much more. Write to:

Llewellyn's *New Worlds of Mind and Spirit*
P.O. Box 64383, Dept. K634-3, St. Paul, MN 55164-0383, U.S.A.

TO ORDER BOOKS AND TAPES

If your book store does not carry the titles described on the following pages, you may order them directly from Llewellyn by sending the full price in U.S. funds, plus postage and handling (see below).

Credit card orders: VISA, MasterCard, American Express are accepted. Call us toll-free within the United States and Canada at 1-800-THE-MOON.

Special Group Discount: Because there is a great deal of interest in group discussion and study of the subject matter of this book, we offer a 20% quantity discount to group leaders or agents. Our Special Quantity Price for a minimum order of five copies of *Psychic Empowerment for Health and Fitness* is $59.55 cash-with-order. Include postage and handling charges noted below.

Postage and Handling: Include $4 postage and handling for orders $15 and under; $5 for orders over $15. There are no postage and handling charges for orders over $100. Postage and handling rates are subject to change. We ship UPS whenever possible within the continental United States; delivery is guaranteed. Please provide your street address as UPS does not deliver to P.O. boxes. Orders shipped to Alaska, Hawaii, Canada, Mexico and Puerto Rico will be sent via first class mail. Allow 4-6 weeks for delivery. International orders: Airmail – add retail price of each book and $5 for each non-book item (audiotapes, etc.); Surface mail – add $1 per item. Minnesota residents add 7% sales tax.

Mail orders to:

Llewellyn Worldwide
P.O. Box 64383, Dept. K634-3, St. Paul, MN 55164-0383, U.S.A.

For customer service, call (612) 291-1970.

Psychic Empowerment
A 7-Day Plan for Self-Development

Joe Slate, Ph.D.

Use 100% of your mind power in just one week! You've heard it before: each of us is filled with an abundance of untapped power—yet we only use one-tenth of its potential. Now a clinical psychologist and famed researcher in parapsychology shows you how to probe your mind's psychic faculties and manifest your capacity to access the higher planes of the mind.

The psychic experience validates your true nature and connects you to your inner knowing. Dr. Slate reveals the life-changing nature of psychic phenomena—including telepathy, out-of-body experiences and automatic writing. At the same time, he shows you how to develop a host of psychic abilities including psychokinesis, crystal gazing, and table tilting.

The final section of the book outlines his accelerated 7-Day Psychic Development Plan through which you can unleash your innate power and wisdom without further delay.

1-56718-635-1, 256 pp., 6 x 9, softcover   **$12.95**

To order, call 1-800-THE-MOON

Prices subject to change without notice.

Psychic Development for Beginners
An Easy Guide to Releasing and Developing
Your Psychic Abilities

William Hewitt

Psychic Development for Beginners provides detailed instruction on developing your sixth sense, or psychic ability. Improve your sense of worth, your sense of responsibility and therefore your ability to make a difference in the world. Innovative exercises like "The Skyscraper" allow beginning students of psychic development to quickly realize personal and material gain through their own natural talent.

Benefits range from the practical to spiritual. Find a parking space anywhere, handle a difficult salesperson, choose a compatible partner, and even access different time periods! Practice psychic healing on pets or humans—and be pleasantly surprised by your results. Use psychic commands to prevent dozing while driving. Preview out-of-body travel, cosmic consciousness and other alternative realities. Instruction in Psychic Development for Beginners is supported by personal anecdotes, 44 psychic development exercises, and 28 related psychic case studies to help students gain a comprehensive understanding of the psychic realm.

1-56718-360-3, 216 pp., 5 1/4 x 8, softcover $9.95

To order, call 1-800-THE-MOON
Prices subject to change without notice.

Yoga for Every Athlete
Secrets of an Olympic Coach

Aladar Kogler, Ph.D.

Whether you train for competition or participate in a sport for the pure pleasure of it, here is a holistic training approach that unifies body and mind through yoga for amazing results. The yoga exercises in this book not only provide a greater sense of well being and deeper unity of body, mind and spirit, they also increase your body's ability to rejuvenate itself for overall fitness.

Use the yoga asanas for warm-up, cool-down, regeneration, compensation of muscle dysbalances, prevention of injuries, stimulation of internal organs, or for increasing your capacity for hard training. You will experience the remarkable benefits of yoga that come from knowing yourself and knowing that you have the ability to control your autonomic, unconscious functions as you raise your mental and physical performance to new heights. Yoga is also the most effective means for accomplishing the daily practice of concentration. Yoga training plans are outlined for 27 different sports.

1-56718-387-5, 320 pp., 6 x 9, softcover   **$16.95**

To order, call 1-800-THE-MOON